Can You Help Me With That?

The Words Every Business Advisor Wants to Hear

By
Business Excellence Partners

Kjell Andreassen
Mary Trost
Chuck Thompson
Mike Tyler
Lynn Whitman

BUSINESS EXCELLENCE

Can You Help Me With That?
Contents

BUSINESSEXCELLENCE

"Can you help me with that?" Words that any business advisor loves to hear....the "Open Sesame" for the advisors' world! Magic Words? Well...not exactly.

Before you hear "Can you help me with that?" from a prospect or client, you will likely have invested quite a lot of resources into achieving that goal. This book will provide a business model for making that investment efficiently and effectively.

So...why read this book? Can you become a successful business advisor without this guide? The answer is yes...you can become a successful business advisor without any help from this book or any other aid, for that matter. You can become a successful business advisor through trial and error. (You could probably become a good surgeon through that method too...however there *are* better ways.) So...why read the book? By implementing the processes and considering the information offered, you will undoubtedly become more successful in a shorter time. Simple as that!

This book was written collaboratively by Business Excellence Partners (BEP), an organization developed by practicing business advisors. The objective of the book is to provide a no-nonsense guide for becoming a successful advisor and bypassing the common mistakes and pitfalls that the partners encountered in the development of their individual practices. Through these experiences, BEP developed a business model that ensures success. Business Excellence Partners was formed with the idea that each of us has skills and perspectives that are different from one another and each of those perspectives offers value to the whole. Kind of like the Chinese proverb "None of us is as smart as all of us". In collaboration, BEP has developed workshops, seminars and other materials, based primarily on the business model, that help both small businesses succeed and business advisors develop successful practices.

Business Excellence Partners consists of five successful business advisors, each accredited by the Institute of Independent Business, a not-for-profit research, training and accreditation organization. (see www.iib.ws). The partners met as members of Arizona Business Advisors, an organization dedicated to collaboration and education for a broad spectrum of business advisors and coaches.

You'll note, in reading this book, that the writing styles and means of presentation of the material are different. Each of the partners has written parts of the book, using their own individual styles and perspectives on the material. As a group, we believe this makes our presentation stronger because of the diversity and broader appeal.
Individually, the partners are:

Kjell Andreassen
Kjell is a Managing Partner of acceler8 llc, a consulting practice focused on business advice, exit planning , tax and accounting. He has extensive experience as an entrepreneur and advisor to a number of emerging and start-up ventures and has held senior executive positions with a number of public and private companies. Kjell is a Certified Exit Planner

(CExP) and Associate Professor at Western International University. He serves as a Mentor for the National Association of Women Business Owners (NAWBO).

Mike Tyler

Mike brings 30 years experience to his work as a business advisor. In leadership roles ranging from *Controller* to *Senior Sales and Marketing Management* to *CEO* and accountability in *North America, Europe* and *Asia*, he brings practical business knowledge across a wide range of subjects. Skilled in strategic planning, mergers & acquisitions, sales and marketing and business analysis, his background is complemented by deep general management experience across a wide range of industry settings.

Chuck Thompson

Chuck is a proven senior executive with over 30 years of accomplishments in the consumer products industry. He has successfully established U.S. based operating companies for European manufacturers and been involved in the successful turn around of several national U.S. companies. Chuck has a strong working knowledge of Sales and Marketing,

Import and Export, Strategic Planning, Inventory management and Retail Operations.

Mary Trost
Mary has been in Senior Executive positions in Nonprofit Organizations for over fifteen years, ten of those as C.E.O. Mary uses her expertise in start up and turn-around to help businesses in a wide variety of industries including the non-profit sector, health services, education, Local Governments, service and retail business, social service, entertainment and tourism. Her Personal and Professional Development Workshops offer a holistic approach to leading full and meaningful business and personal lives.

Lynn Whitman
Lynn has a track record of providing small businesses with creative solutions for success. She spent 25 years in senior management in the department store business and several years as COO of a promotional marketing consortium. She has background in finance, credit card management and marketing. She serves as a mentor and leads an entrepreneurial group for Fresh Start Women's Foundation.

If you still aren't convinced that this book is worth the price or the time, consider that the business model offered here is unique. You won't find this model in a business class at the local college. You won't find this in a trade organization. You won't find this in one of the online "How to become a business advisor in 3 easy steps" websites. This proven model for a successful business advisory practice is available in this book and an expanded version in the Business Excellence Academy ONLY.

What makes this model so special? The answer is <u>reality</u>. In all, our model for the advisory business is realistic. By knowing the pitfalls to avoid and the short-cuts to take, you are assured a better shot at a successful practice.

If you finish this book and want to know more, email us at info@businessexcellencepartners.com

BUSINESSEXCELLENCE

Chapter 1 – The Business Model
By Mike Tyler

What are Business Models and why we need them?

This book is not about business models in general, but one model in particular. It's a proprietary model, developed by Business Excellence Partners (BEP) that allows business advisors to develop a sustainable, successful practice. It will lead to clients asking the question we all love to hear – "Can you help me with that?"

There are a plethora of books and articles on the different types and respective merits of the hundreds of models currently in use, with more being invented daily, and with more definitions than anyone can handle.

For our purposes we can use this simple definition to illustrate what it is:

A business model dictates the way in which a company fulfills its activities and allows it to create a sustainable profitable enterprise.

How much does the Business Advisor need to know about Models?

It's fair to say that the practitioner will need more than a rudimentary knowledge of the main business models and how they can influence growth and profitability. Each client's business will be different but having a well thought out business model is a prerequisite to strategy development and implementation.

Stories and examples abound about "game changing" models, such as Southwest Airlines which began in the 1970's with a revolutionary new "low cost business model for airlines" and today carries more passengers than any other airline worldwide. Southwest focused on just one airplane, the Boeing 737 to minimize maintenance costs and only flew short, direct flights to secondary (less costly) airports moving away from the established norm in the airline industry of the "hub and spoke" model. They combined this low cost model with a customer care culture that encouraged employees and customers to "lighten up" and have some fun- the result is history. Game changing models may be few and far between but there are lessons to be learned from their application and the advisor would be well placed to familiarize themselves with the main types of business models and how they may be applied to small businesses.

Does the need for a business model apply to me?

Many advisors describe themselves as being "generalists" having had a broad business background; this is indeed a good thing, however can result in a lack of focus, as the advisor tends to try to do everything themselves, resulting in a less than optimum implementation for the client and poor productivity for the advisor.

The advisor needs to identify their core strengths and focus on those as they develop their strategy and marketing efforts; a well thought out business model is a key component in developing a sustainable, successful practice.

Business Excellence Partners Business Model– Developed by Advisors for Advisors

The BEP Business Model has been developed based on the successful practices used by a number of advisors over a number of years – put simply, it has proven successful in developing and growing business advisor practices that are sustainable over time. The model encompasses three distinct phases.

Phase 1
No Vacancy – Fully Booked

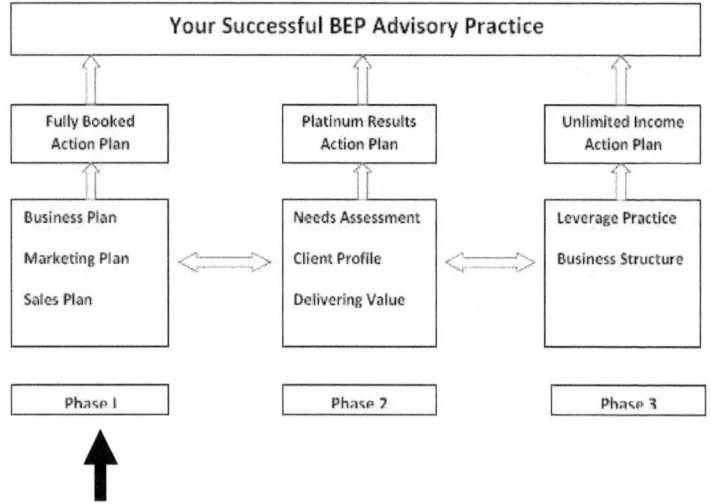

The first phase is focused on acquiring and keeping clients and ensuring that the advisor is as busy as they want to be; most practitioners have experienced the "feast or famine' situation common in this industry and this section addresses the key actions to be taken to avoid this. It literally means that the advisor has a constant stream of opportunities and clients and consequently can declare themselves to be "fully booked

This phase is about developing structure and laying out a road map that is a guide to growing and improving your practice. As with any business the fundamentals of success are based on developing and implementing a business plan, a marketing plan and a sales plan and each of these is covered in detail in a subsequent chapter.

Acquiring clients

Acquiring clients is a process that can be followed by anyone and is of particular use to those individuals who find the sales and marketing process difficult, uncomfortable or even tedious. Ensuring a steady pipeline of business will avoid the famine or feast situation endemic to the advisor industry and is ably demonstrated in the marketing and sales chapters.

Identifying your focus areas

Furthermore, determining what your core strengths are, what you enjoy doing and what is profitable for you is a key part of building your success platform; we call this "Identifying your Hot Spot" and will be covered in a later chapter.

Building trust

A final word in this section must emphasize the importance of building trust to the longevity of client relationships; without this, assignments become a series of projects and the opportunities for building a reputation and receiving referrals becomes more limited.
We'll explore in depth the key ingredients for building trust and for utilizing it to grow your practice.

Phase 2
U Rock – Platinum Results

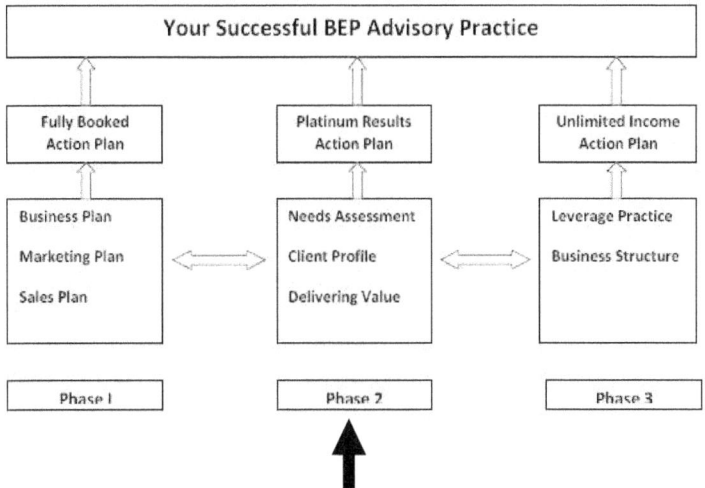

The second phase concentrates on how to deliver value to clients, ultimately one of the critical components for success. We want our advisors to appear as "Rockstars" in the eyes of their clients and the results they deliver to exceed expectations. The content and quality of BEP's support tools and processes will ensure the reputation of the advisor.

The second phase focuses on delivering superior value to your clients, what we call "platinum results". You must be able to have an immediate and visible impact on your clients in two key areas: saving them time and money.

Understanding the Environment
The environment in which the small business owner operates is very different from the corporate experience that most advisors have undergone. Many businesses are family owned with additional needs and issues that have to be considered. There will be less structure and process and the advisor will need to carefully manage the client engagement in order to take account of all these diverse issues.
Having the ability to "put yourselves in their shoes" and subvert your own ego and experience is a critical skill set if the advisor is to be successful in delivering real value; you'll read how to do this in Chapter 7.

Where do I start?
It would be nice if there was a pre- arranged road map, which had been developed together by the advisor and the client, and which could be used to prioritize the different work areas. The bad news is there isn't one, but the good news is you can develop one! In fact it

becomes essential to do so, to ensure that you are working on the right things; it also provides a measurement base for demonstrating value delivered to your client. BEP has a proprietary business assessment tool that does all of the above things, providing a method for effective client management; it can also be a very effective tool in acquiring new clients.

Delivering Value
Your ability to deliver value depends on a number of diverse factors some of which will be under your control and some of which may not. For example client receptivity can be a difficult challenge to overcome and will depend on your ability to demonstrate that your recommendations are valid. Collaboration with other advisors is an important element in delivering value, as they provide not only additional credibility, but expert specialist skills which you may not possess.
Delivering value depends not only on providing and developing superior business ideas, but also in assisting in their implementation, and here again there may be factors outside your

control such as financing needs, timing issues, workload and competing projects.

In summary your ability to deliver value will require a well thought out approach that includes a collaborative network of support resources. You can read more on this subject under Chapter 9.

Phase 3
Grand Slam- Unlimited Income

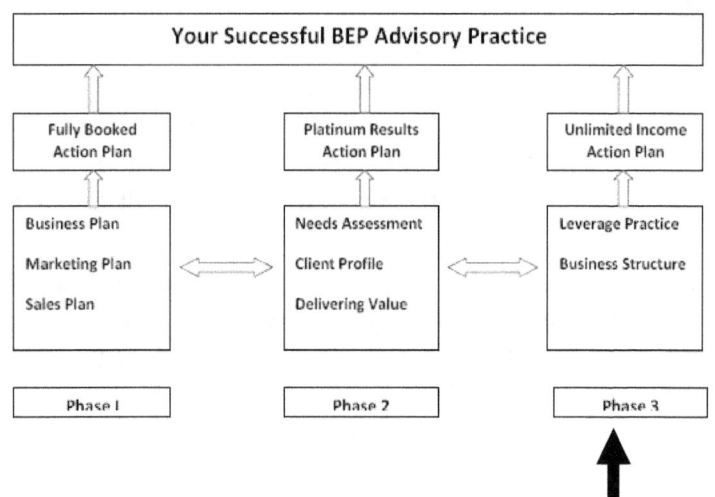

So you've done everything right so far and you've got the bases loaded! What else do you need to do to get that Grand Slam? This

section addresses effective implementation through structure and leverage which will allow you to maximize your time and income.
This third and final phase is about some of the practical aspects of structuring and leveraging your practice so that your time, and subsequently income, is optimized.
Here again BEP has a number of proprietary tools that are designed to enable you to do scenario planning about the impact of different options available to you.

Legal and Administrative Issues
Business Excellence Partners can lead you through some of the intricacies involved in structuring the right type of practice, including legal structure, physical surroundings, support tools and processes and communication systems. These can be very time consuming and can often lead to the wrong structures being established with serious consequences.

Leveraging Your Practice
Our focus here is on developing multiple sources of income streams, necessary to protect cash flow against the 'famine or feast' type situation which many advisors run up against.

A key component of this involves collaborating with other BEP advisors to jointly service clients or develop new offerings; every single practitioner is limited by available hours and collaboration allows them to leverage their position and practice into something bigger than they can provide as an individual.
BEP participants will use a planning tool to map out how their income streams will look and what needs to be put in place in order to maintain them.

A final word on the business model, before we delve more into the details; using this model will provide a structure and a roadmap which have proven to be the key ingredients in developing successful and sustainable practices. Can you start a practice without it? Yes you can, but you critically endanger your chance of success by doing so.
With a trial and error approach you may eventually find the right path, or you may not, and you will have used up a lot of time looking.

Using the model together with attaining the CBeA certification from the Business Excellence Workshops is the first step toward a successful practice.

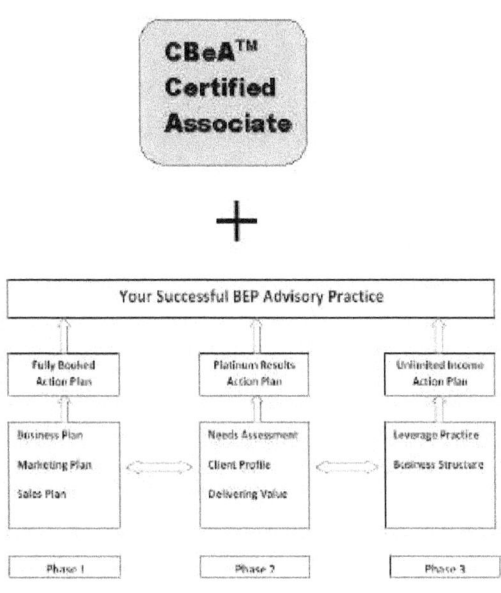

BUSINESSEXCELLENCE

Chapter 2 – The Business Plan
By Mike Tyler

The Business Plan Dilemma

Do you see a correlation between these two statements?

- *More than 75% of all small businesses do not have a business plan that guides how they run their business*
- *80 % of all small businesses fail within 5 years*

There is indeed a strong correlation - the lack of business planning, and its effective implementation is the most important factor in explaining the high failure rate. Not having a business plan is akin to going on a vacation to Hawaii without booking the airplane and hotels – very few would think of doing that, so it's not clear why so many business owners do not develop a plan. It may well be something they intend to do but get distracted by working "in the business" instead of "on the business".

The BEP Business Model
Chapter 1 discussed the need for a business model and developing a plan is the first step of Phase I of the Model – No Vacancy, Fully Booked

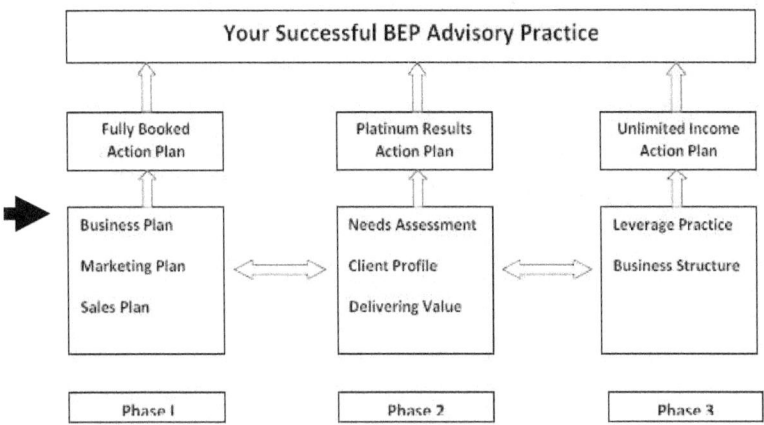

What will be included in my plan, and what will I use it for?
At BEP we have developed an approach that involves putting together a high level business plan that sets an overall direction and identifies operating options; it also identifies strengths

and weaknesses and, crucially, identifies the support resources you'll need to implement your plan.

The purpose of this high level plan is to describe your objectives in a number of different areas. You'll also assess your ability to fulfill them, taking account of your skills and available resources. This plan will guide you as you develop more detailed marketing and sales plans and identify the key issues that you'll need to address in order to be successful.

The Planning Cycle

In putting together your plan you will need to look at 5 key areas, which will form the basis for your financial plan, as outlined below:

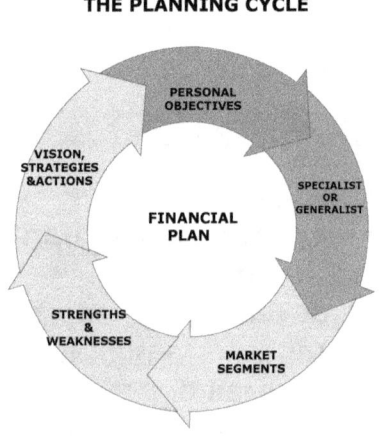

THE PLANNING CYCLE

Personal Objectives
Executives decide to pursue this opportunity for a whole variety of reasons such as:
- Supplementing existing income
- Main source of income
- Staying involved and engaged
- Sharing knowledge/giving back
- Building a network
- Looking for investment or employment opportunities

Understanding your primary motives will help determine how to construct your business plan and subsequent activities.

Time and Resource Allocation
Determining how much time you want to allocate to your business again may well dictate the approach you take. Similarly, identifying the cash resources you have available to invest will help to frame your objectives. In addition you may have cash needs that your business is going to have to provide and these need to be identified and quantified.
.

Advisor Focus
The basic choices here focus around being a generalist or a specialist, or some combination of both. This may apply both functionally and by industry; an Associate may well have a specialty that can be also be of use to other Associates. In addition they may have contacts within a particular industry that will provide opportunities.
Note also that the specialist advisor can fulfill the role of the generalist to their clients by utilizing the services of other Associates.

Target Market Segment(s)
The largest segment is the small business owner who covers different industries, and this segment is very applicable for the generalist advisor. By and large this segment falls in a range of companies who have sales of between $0.5 million and $20 million.
Other segments may be good targets based on the Associate's background and network.

Strengths and Weaknesses
The primary purpose is to identify opportunities to provide service to other Associates and to identify skill gaps that will need support and collaboration from others.

BEP has partnered with The Carefree Institute to provide an assessment tool (The Inner View) (http://bepinnerview.blogspot.com/) that can be used to help the advisor identify these strengths and weaknesses and to use them as a basis for their marketing and sales efforts.

Vision, Mission, Strategy and Actions

Developing a Vision will enable you to see what an end result looks like, given a specified time period. It should be challenging, but realistic and should specify the geographies in which you'll operate, the markets you will focus on, together with the products and services you will offer.

A Mission statement needs to look at things from your customers' viewpoint and should lay out what products and services you provide and what benefits they will derive from them. Strategies and actions are the way to fulfill your vision and mission and will be incorporated in the work you do to develop your sales and marketing plans covered in Chapters 3 through 6.

Financial Plan

Business Excellence Partners has developed a planning tool (http://businessexcellenceworkshops.blogspot.com/) that members of the Academy can use to forecast and fine tune their business. (Also available for purchase). It also indicates the resources and personal effort that will be needed to develop and maintain certain levels of income.

This is a critical issue for the rookie advisor as most people significantly underestimate the time and effort required to develop a sustainable income stream.

As a minimum, anyone considering entering this field should ensure that they have set aside enough income to last for a six to 12 month period while they are building their practice- the reason most businesses fail is lack of planning and lack of cash and it's no different for the business advisor.

Summary

Completing this high level plan will allow the advisor to focus on the areas where they will be the most likely to succeed, as well as establishing a sound framework from which to build their detailed marketing and sales activities. The chances of success are greatly enhanced by following this well tested approach.

BUSINESSEXCELLENCE

Chapter 3 – Marketing Your Practice
The Best, Most Effective and Proven Strategies and Tactics to get FULLY BOOKED
By: Kjell Andreassen, AInstIB, CExP
Introduction:

Objective of this chapter:
To generate a personalized marketing plan for your practice, packed with proven tools and techniques to be Fully Booked – No Vacancy; a constant stream of opportunities and clients. A marketing plan that is focused on consistency and a sustainable effort allows you to:
- Generate prospects and clients efficiently and at a lower per unit cost
- Remain focused, with your goals and vision in mind, without distractions caused by short term marketing bursts
- Get in the minds of your targets so they will think of you more often

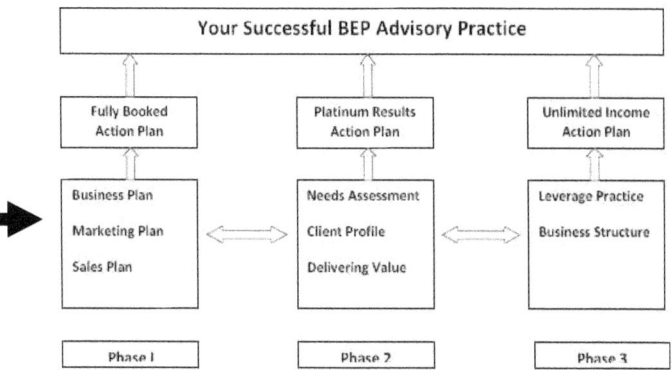

Your marketing foundation:

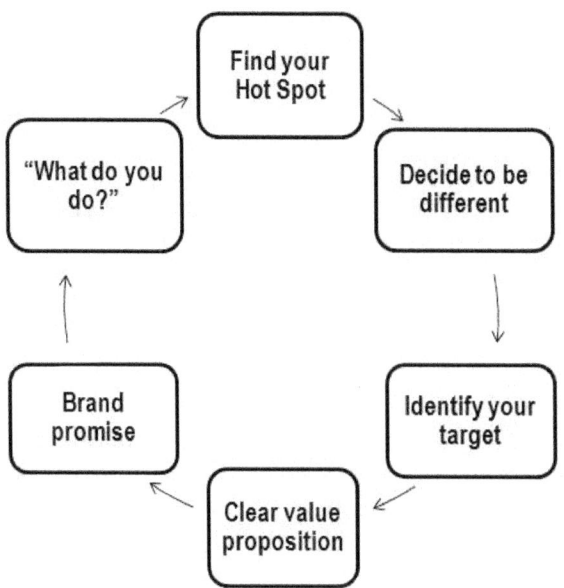

Find Your Hot Spot:
The key to developing your branding strategy and building your marketing plan is to define your Brand as the basis for your differentiation strategy. You already know that there are thousands of business owners out there that need your help, prospective clients that with your help and guidance can enhance the success of their business. You know what it takes and you have the skills and abilities to create real value for the client. This is the basis for crafting your value proposition – but first ask yourself: why should they choose you? What sets you apart from the many sources of assistance that are out there? Coupled with this is the need to emphasize what you enjoy doing and what can be most profitable for your practice.

In terms of your practice, if time, energy or money was not the issue, what could you be one of the very best at? What are your most exceptional skills and talents? Start by listing what you are really good at. Be careful to not fall in the trap that thinking that just because it comes easy to you, it is easy for everyone else. I have often found that where I add the most value to a client is by doing some of the things that come naturally to me, that I find easy, but the client just does not know how to attack or solve – like crafting a good value proposition, creating good measurable written objectives or identifying the USP (Unique Selling Proposition) for a client.

Second, think about what you do in your practice and list what activities you enjoy the most. Often, what you do with true passion is what sets you apart – passion is contagious and passion sells – passion (or the lack of it!) is transmitted through everything you do, how you do it and how you communicate what you do.

Third, ask yourself what are the tasks or actions that you perform in your practice that generate the most opportunities or direct billings? What are the most profitable actions or programs that you provide?

Now, compare the three lists and look for overlap between items on the list of what you are the best at and what you most enjoy doing. Then, from that list of overlap, find what overlaps with the list of the actions and programs that generate the most opportunities or revenue.

You have now identified the basis for your Hot Spot! Build a brand and a marketing plan that supports you spending as much time as possible working in your Hot Spot – make this your Brand and your Differentiator!

Define your Hot Spot Target
Use the results from your Hot Spot analysis above and identify your target customers. Be specific and narrow this down as much as

possible. A target market that is too broad makes it harder for others to relate to what you do and it is harder to refer prospects to you. Do not fall in the trap of thinking that by being too narrow you might miss out on business opportunities outside of your target market – differentiation is the key – focus on your Hot Spot. Keep in mind that by becoming a big fish in a small pond (your Hot Spot or niche) you will often be asked to come and swim in other ponds.

Who are the groups who use the services you provide? Which of these groups do you most relate to or feel the most excitement about working with? Which groups do you already have clients in and have the most knowledge about?

What sets you apart?
Use your Hot Spot analysis to determine a relevant and differentiating position for your brand. Make sure to base this on something the client cares about, but also something that sets you apart from competition. Decide to be different!

Create your brand promise
Make a promise to your clients, based on your values and your differentiating position –

describe the emotional benefits of your brand. Remember, it is not about what you do or how you do it – it is all about benefits, often emotional benefits, resulting from what you do for your clients. For the business owner this is often tied to more sales, more profits, better cash flow or more time with their family – not strategies or business plans (even though this is what you do and what will get the client to the emotional benefits). Remember, the client's decision to retain your services is based on emotion, not logic. They will find the logic to support the emotional decision they want to make!

Once you make a promise, you will need to deliver on this promise – all that you do should be designed to deliver on your promise every day in every way. Remember that your brand is only as good as your client's last experience!

What do you do?
This is probably the question that you come across most frequently whenever you engage in networking or relationship building and marketing your practice. By crafting a succinct answer to this question and basing the content

on the analysis above, you will further enhance the basis for your branding and marketing. You now know your hot spot, your target, what makes you different and your brand promise. Use this to define what the key problems faced by your target market are. How do you solve these problems and present unique (differentiation) solutions to your clients? What are the most dramatic results that you have achieved and what are the benefits to your clients. Explain in your answer who you work with (your target market), what their problems are, how you solve these problems and the results that you achieve and how this benefits your customer. You now have a basis for formulating your branding statement, your USP (Unique Selling Proposition), to answer the question "What do you do?" and your 30 second commercial or elevator speech. Most importantly, you are ready to define your brand.

Define Your Brand
Your Brand is the complete collection of all experiences and impressions of who you are and what you do, on a continued and consistent basis. Your Brand is your marketing foundation, consisting of the most important

ingredients in creating the right impression of
your practice:

- A clear and consistent message –
  your Brand
- Logo and stationery
- Well defined visual presentations of
  your services and your service
  process
- A customized and well designed
  website
- A customized and well designed
  brochure

Unfortunately, this is where many begin – by
creating brochures, designing logos and
business cards and building the website.
However, this is not the place to start. If you
have not completed the steps above first, save
your money!
Armed with a clear definition of:

- Your Hot Spot
- Your target
- Your differentiators
- Your brand promise
- Your "What do you do" statement

you can now clearly define your branding
strategy. You have all that you need to design
a clear and concise marketing message, design
a logo, stationary, and business cards, develop
an appropriate content for a brochure and for

your website – all reflecting your branding strategy, brand promise, value proposition, benefits and differentiators. Your practice has an identity that clearly communicates what you can do for your clients – it is easy to relate to, and clients, prospects and referral partners understand what you do, the value that you bring and why they should do business with **you.**

You can now develop the tactical areas in your marketing plan, choose and develop the strategies that you will employ, all consistently communicating your brand.

Use your marketing foundation to promote your practice:

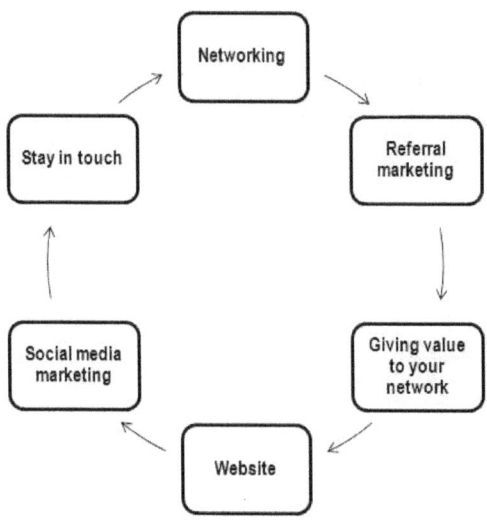

Promoting your practice

Getting "Fully Booked – No Vacancy", requires a consistent and deliberate execution of strategies and tactics designed to promote your practice, build trust and reputation and maintain a constant presence in front of your target market in the community that you serve. Based on your strengths and capabilities, pick the strategies that you feel, over time, work best for you. This chapter covers some of the key strategies that have consistently delivered results for the advisors of Business Excellence Partners. Combine these with more traditional selling methods, or other strategies that you feel will complement your strengths. In the other chapters book, you can read more about relationship selling and building trust, both critical supporting complements in getting to No Vacancy – Fully Booked.

The marketing plan for your practice should include programs promoting your practice by
- Deliberate and consistent networking
- Focused and consistent referral marketing
- Leveraging your website and social media marketing opportunities

- Consistently staying in touch

Complement this by including blogging, public speaking, publishing, direct mail, cold calling or other methods based on your strengths and interests.

Networking and referrals

Start by leveraging your existing network. Referrals are based on visibility and trust. Within your existing network you already have visibility, they know who you are, and you probably also have a certain level of trust.   If you are just starting your practice, send out a "birth announcement card" to your entire network – you will be amazed as to how many will think of you or get back in touch after hearing from you and learning about your new venture.

Expanding your network and creating visibility and trust requires time and effort – so it is important to work from a plan that is goal oriented, consistent and deliberate. Attending meetings and collecting or distributing business cards, without a clear goal in mind and without clear strategies for follow up, rarely leads to anything more than wasting a lot of your time and money.

First, identify networking organizations that serve your target market. Keep in mind that your first objective is not necessarily to meet prospects or try to sell your service. No one likes to be sold. Instead look for others that serve the same target market as you do – look for referral sources rather than prospects. Think of a networking event as a place to make connections with people, people with whom you can develop relationships and trust, expand your network and gain referrals. Meeting and building a relationship with one referral source at a networking event can be very valuable, much more so than just identifying a potential prospect. Go to the event with a specific goal in mind, for example finding a business attorney, a CPA or a Financial Planner that works with business owners. Rather than just "working the room" on a random basis, ask the event leader or the greeter at the door to point you in the direction of someone that fits your goal. Approach targets with a mindset of finding how you can best help this person, not how to sell yourself and what you do. If you first focus on finding targeted referral sources and then on how you can best help these individuals, you will quickly build relationships and gain trust – by giving! Giving is also, for many of us, much more fun than selling yourself. Consistent giving is the best basis for obtaining consistent referral results. There are excellent books available on the topic of generating business by referral. Do not assume that you know how to do this because you have been doing this your entire career – take time to read up on the subject and learn the methods that work when applied consistently.

Referral marketing and networking take time and patience. When you have identified networking groups or leads groups that appear to be a good fit, give it at least 6 months to a year, with consistent presence, to determine if they are the right organizations for you. Get involved in a committee or find other ways to gain visibility and credibility with the group. Focus more on identifying prospective referral sources than on identifying prospects. Once a potential referral partner has been identified, focus on developing a deep relationship and trust. Educate your network and your referral partner so they have a very clear understanding of what you do – that way they will be in a better position to find good, qualified leads or prospects for you. This takes time and a commitment from both parties to invest the time to learn about each others' business. Someone who is not willing to make this investment is probably not a good referral partner candidate. A deliberate program of giving includes finding referrals for your referral partners, finding ways to promote them to others and making them look good without worrying about what you get in return. If you focus on building good referral relationships and giving value to your network, your phone will start ringing, guaranteed!

Leverage your website and social media marketing opportunities
Build a quality website by using a professional web designer. It is not about cool looks and spectacular animation – it is all about communication. Your website should clearly communicate your value proposition and lend credibility to your practice. Use client testimonials and case studies showcasing your results to add credibility to your website. You have just a few seconds to communicate two critical items: What is your value proposition, and who says so?
Once your website is up, make sure to get listed in search engines and optimize your site. Identify the key words appropriate to your practice and your value proposition. Get some advice on how best to optimize; it does not

have to cost much to be effective. Identify the use of social media that can enhance your internet presence. Remember, you will have an online reputation whether you like it or not – do what you can to enhance your online reputation. Use of social media tactics can be very time consuming and sometimes overwhelming. Select what can best work for you. If you find the technical aspects of this intimidating, collaborate with others that have the talent and knowledge. All social media tactics work together. It is the synergy of everything combined that brings clients to your business and gives you credibility. Whether it is LinkedIn, Twitter, Facebook, Yelp or any of the other social media available, or your own personal blog – develop a strong content strategy that will drive traffic to your central hub of information, usually your website or your blog. On your blog or website, create a professional online presence for your unique skill set. Provide tips and useful resources to build skills within your area of expertise. Keep everything current and update on a regular basis.

Create a social media business plan identifying your objectives for each tool and identify the time that you are willing to commit. Search the web on a regular basis to monitor your name, blogs and markets; collect useful information for your blog. Build community participation by building a strong social media network; create presence in communities linked to your business objectives. Consider developing micro sites to increase awareness of individual service offerings.

Stay in touch with your clients and your network.
Every week/month that you are not in touch with your clients or your network your credibility drops. Customers who have not heard from you for a while are much more likely to go to someone else, referral sources that have not heard from you in a while are much more likely to refer to someone else. Create a plan that will maintain contact with you entire network, clients and prospects on a consistent basis. Make sure that your contact methods are designed to give value and deepen or maintain the relationships. The methods are many; I recommend that you meet, in person, with your most trusted referral partners and deepest relationships on a regular basis. Use the phone, e-mail, thank-you cards, written notes or newsletters. Forward an article of interest, make a referral,

invite someone to a networking event. Pick the tools that fit best for you; the keys are consistency and that the content that you use provides value and is relevant and interesting. The goal is to keep your name in front of your network and position your name and your brand as the expert in your field.

Summary
To build a practice that is Fully Booked – No Vacancy, create a marketing plan that is focused on generating clients and prospects on a consistent and sustainable basis, while getting your name in the minds of your targets so they will think of you more often.

Your marketing foundation:
- Identify your Hot Spot
- Decide to be different
- Identify your target
- Define a clear value proposition
- Define your brand promise (value and benefits)
- Refine your "what do you do" statement

Use your marketing foundation to promote your practice:
- Deliberate and consistent networking

- Focused and consistent referral marketing
- Give value to your network consistently
- Leverage your website and social media marketing opportunities
- Stay in touch – consistently and deliberately

BUSINESS EXCELLENCE

Chapter 4- Relationship Selling
By Chuck Thompson

Success or failure as a Business Advisor often hinges on your ability to develop strong relationships with your clients. Relationships lead to repeat assignments and often lead to referrals; your best source of new business. But, what is the key to developing strong relationships? The answer lies in understanding the characteristics of the different kinds of relationships. That is what we will explore in this chapter.

Relationship selling is an important element of your Sales Plan. Referring back to The Business Excellence Model, your Sales Plan is an essential element in reaching the goal of "No Vacancy", ensuring that your practice remains always "Fully Booked."

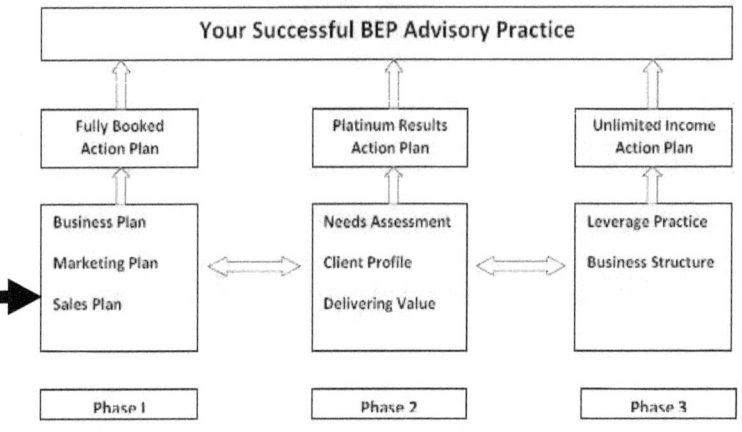

In order to understand the various types of relationships as they pertain to the selling process I have broadly grouped them into four main areas based upon the needs of the client. The four areas that we will explore are: relationships based strictly on **Service**; relationships based on client **Needs**; relationships based on **On-going Relationships**; and relationships based on **Trust**.

The relationship approach that you, as a Business Advisor, decide to utilize will largely determine the nature of your individual

practice. None is right or wrong. But the end
results are vastly different.

The Service Based Relationship

In a Service Based Relationship, the Business
Advisor offers a service to clients. The service
is not generally tailored to the clients'
individual needs. Rather, the service is
something of broad appeal that can be useful
to many different types of clients. It is often
characterized by being timely in nature;
addressing a particular business opportunity or
societal problem that may currently exist. As
an example, in difficult economic times, the
Business Advisor might focus on assisting
clients in obtaining financing, SBA loans or
grants. Often the client will have no prior
relationship with the Business Advisor and will
become aware of the Business Advisor when
searching for help or solutions to a specific
problem. Once the service is provided, the
client may or may not use the services of the
Business Advisor again.

In this type of relationship, the focus is on
providing information to clients. Business

Advisors often find clients for the service that they are offering through group meetings or seminars. Their time is spent explaining the details or benefits of the service that they are offering, rather than on uncovering the specific needs of the client.

Advisory practices built on this type of approach rely heavily on finding new and timely services to offer. They constantly seek ways to market their offering to a large number of potential clients. Success is largely determined by their ability to consistently draw large audiences to attend their seminars or product presentations. In short, it is a numbers game. If you reach enough people, someone will buy. Success is determined by knowing how many potential clients must be reached to sell the offering.

The Needs Based Relationship

From time to time, all businesses encounter problems when operating their business. Many look to the Business Advisor for help in solving the specific problem encountered. This is a needs based relationship in its simplest form. The client has a problem. The Business Adviser is hired to solve the problem. When the client receives a solution to the problem, the relationship is usually ended. Because of the narrow focus of the service offered, in most cases, clients do not have the ability to work regularly with the Advisor.

Business Advisors who build their practice on solving client needs often specialize in specific areas. They try to develop a reputation of expertise in a given field. For example, a Business Advisor may focus strictly on IT problems, or Human Resource problems, or Labor Negotiation, or Sales and Marketing. The fields of possible emphasis are many, with many more opportunities within each area.

Successful Business Advisors who build their practice on needs based relationships often find that it is most effective to concentrate on a narrow niche within a field. By doing so, this enables them to more easily develop a reputation as a specialist in the chosen field.

Marketing a needs based practice differs greatly from the previous service based practice that we discussed. A needs based practice, because of it narrow focus, benefits more from referrals, networking and collaboration with other advisors.

The Relationship Based Relationship

One of the biggest challenges that every Business Advisor faces is developing a needed level of business that is sustainable in the future. Developing client relationships will lead to repeat business. And, repeat business is an essential element in developing a level of business that is sustainable and predictable in the future.

A relationship practice strives to build repeat business through in depth analysis of the client's organization. The Business Advisor spends time studying the client's organization looking for possible problem areas or areas of inefficiency. The Advisor then provides the client with ideas and possible solutions to help the organization function more smoothly. In this type of relationship, the client benefits from the Advisor's knowledge and previous experience. And, often, the Advisor is asked by the client to help solve problem areas, that prior to the Advisor's review, the client did not realize existed.

Over time, the Advisor can become a valuable "partner" in the client's business because of the Advisor's thorough understanding of the client's business. Advisor's who use this approach to building their business also rely heavily on referrals. Their focus centers on developing long term relationships with their clients. Clients are then encouraged to refer the Advisor to other business associates.

When starting to work with a new client, Advisors will often use a Business Assessment Tool, such as the one available through Business Excellence Partners, to help evaluate the various areas of the business. The deficiencies uncovered will then provide a good starting point for building a strong client – advisor working relationship.

The Trust Based Relationship

A relationship based practice often leads to a Trust Based relationship between the client and the Business Advisor. In a trust based relationship the focus shifts from the needs of the client's organization to the personal needs of the client. The Advisor invests time and energy in trying to understand the client and his personal goals, desires, strengths and weaknesses.

In this type of relationship, the Advisor is no longer just a business associate. The Advisor has moved on to become a Trusted Advisor and has earned the personal trust of the client. The Advisor becomes a safe haven when difficult issues must be discussed and difficult decisions made.

A clear sign that the relationship has moved to this level is when the client regularly asks the Advisor "Can you help me with that?" -- a phrase essential to all Advisors wishing to center their practice on repeat business.

A Trust based practice centers on building long term relationships with clients. The Advisor relies on referrals and collaboration for future growth, but the majority of the business of the practice comes from repeat business with existing clients.

The following chart summarizes the four different types of relationships that we have discussed.

Characteristics of Different Client Relationships

	Focus Is On	Energy Spent On	Client Receives	Indicators of Success
Service Based	Answers, Expertise, Input	Explaining	Information	Timely, High Quality Deliverables
Needs Based	Business Problem	Problem Solving	Solutions	Problems Resolved
Relationship Based	Client Organization	Providing Insights	Ideas	Repeat Business
Trust Based	Client As Individual	Understanding The Client	Safe Haven For Hard Issues	Personal Trust

Adapted by Michael Leeman (http://theleemangroup.com) from David H. Maister, Charles H. Green & Robert M. Galford, *The Trusted Advisor* (Free Press, 2001)

The Trusted Advisor

Becoming a trusted advisor is essential to building an on-going, sustainable advisory practice that has predicable annual income. Understanding what it takes to become a Trusted Advisor is important since most successful advisors who choose to follow this path exhibit similar characteristics.

Trusted Advisors….

- Focus on the client, rather than themselves.
- Focus on the client as an individual, not as a person fulfilling a role.
- Believe that a continued focus on problem definition and resolution is more important than technical or content mastery.
- Show a strong "competitive" drive aimed not at competitors, but at constantly finding new ways to be of greater service to the client.
- Consistently focus on doing the next right thing, rather than on aiming for specific outcomes.
- Are motivated more by an internalized drive to do the right thing than by their own organization's rewards or dynamics.
- View methodologies, models, techniques, and business processes as means to an end.
- Believe that success in client relationships is tied to the accumulation of quality experiences.
- Believe that both selling and serving are aspects of professionalism.

- Believe that there is a distinction between a business life and a private life, but that both lives are personal.
- Believe the ultimate sign of trust is "Can You Help Me With That".

Summary

The business model that has been developed by Business Excellence Partners provides a proven format for developing and sustaining your Business Advisory practice. As the model indicates, an effective Sales Plan is one of the first things that must be accomplished.

Sales can be achieved in many different ways. The goal of the Business Excellence Partners Model is to develop a Plan that is sustainable and that will keep your practice "Fully Booked".

In our opinion, this is best achieved through building a practice centered on becoming a Trusted Advisor to your clients. This approach provides the greatest opportunity to gain business through referrals and through collaboration with other Advisors, two key elements to growing a practice that will continue to provide rewards in the future.

The relationship approach that you ultimately decide upon will determine the path you will need to follow to get clients. The Trusted Advisor approach will make that task

BUSINESSEXCELLENCE

Chapter 5- The Sales Process
By Chuck Thompson

All businesses rely on sales for their survival. Businesses may differ in the number of customers that they need, the types of products or services that they supply, or whether their focus is on new sales or long range relationships. But, in the end, they all need sales to bring in the revenue necessary to support operations.

How businesses get sales may differ also. However, the sales process itself follows the same logical stages regardless of the type of sale being made. And, this sales process is the same for the Business Advisor. Understanding the sales cycle and how it works is an important first step to developing an effective

Sales Plan for your Business Advisory practice. As we discussed in the previous chapter, preparing a Sales Plan that is thorough and sustainable is one of the core elements of our proven business model.

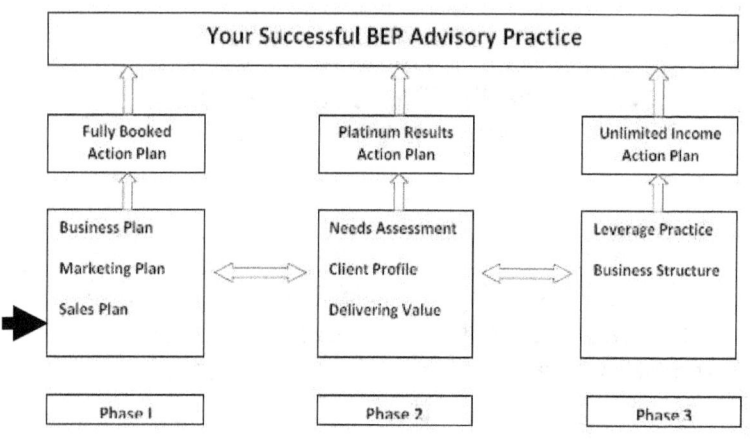

All businesses rely on sales for their survival. Businesses may differ in the number of customers that they need, the types of products or services that they supply, or whether their focus is on new sales or long range relationships. But, in the end, they all need sales to bring in the revenue necessary to support operations.

How businesses get sales may differ also. However, the sales process itself follows the same logical stages regardless of the type of sale being made. And, this sales process is the same for the Business Advisor. Understanding the sales cycle and how it works is an important first step to developing an effective Sales Plan for your Business Advisory practice. As we discussed in the previous chapter, preparing a Sales Plan that is thorough and sustainable is one of the core elements of our proven business model.

The Sales Process

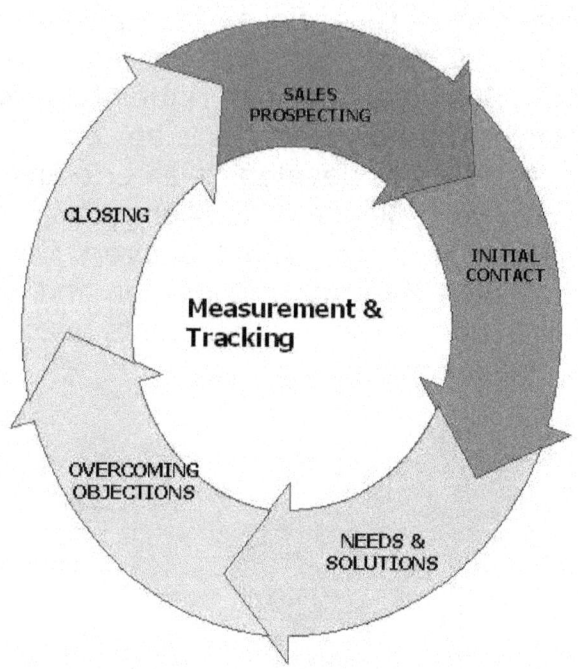

The final stage in the sales process is *Tracking*. This is a stage that is often overlooked. It is also a stage that is essential to understanding that the sales process is ongoing and cannot be allowed to be interrupted if success is to be achieved.

Sales Prospecting

Finding new clients or customers is the life blood of any business and that is certainly true for the Business Adviser as well. If you are starting a new business or practice the need to find new customers is immediately apparent. Without customers there will be no sales revenue.

For established businesses the need is often less apparent. But, it is still there. Established businesses lose customers regardless of their efforts to keep them. Customers go out of business; they merge with other companies; they decide to work with your competition etc. The sales volume that is lost must be replaced if growth is going to continue and your company is going to survive.

Remember that our goal is a "Fully Booked" practice. To achieve that, seeking new clients must be a part of each day's activities.

Sales Prospecting

Finding new clients or customers is the life blood of any business and that is certainly true for the Business Adviser as well. If you are starting a new business or practice the need to find new customers is immediately apparent. Without customers there will be no sales revenue.

For established businesses the need is often less apparent. But, it is still there. Established businesses lose customers regardless of their efforts to keep them. Customers go out of business; they merge with other companies; they decide to work with your competition etc. The sales volume that is lost must be replaced if growth is going to continue and the company is going to survive.

Remember that our goal is a "Fully Booked" practice. To achieve that, seeking new clients must be a part of each day's activities.

So, how do companies or Business Advisors find new clients? The answers are many. Some businesses use direct mail. Others use telemarketing. Some use e mail blasts. Some find trade shows most effective. Some use door to door cold calling. Others rely exclusively on referrals. There is no one right answer, and the method used may change as the business grows and develops.

The chart below shows one method that can be used to decide the approach that may be best for you.

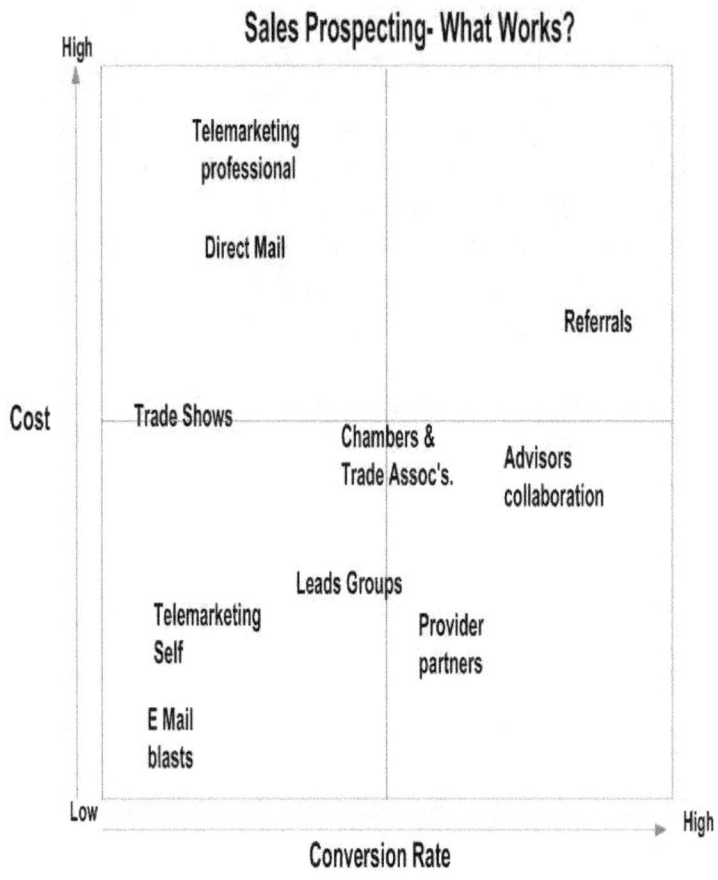

Sales Prospecting- What Works?

As this chart indicates, the axis on the left indicates the Cost and Time involved going from low to high. The axis along the bottom of the chart indicates the Conversion Rate going from low to high.

Activities found in the upper left hand area of the chart have a relatively high cost and a low conversion rate. Activities found in the lower right hand area of the chart have a high conversion rate with a relatively low cost.

For the purpose of discussion, we have included some possible prospecting activities into the chart. Depending on the business, prospecting activities and associated costs may differ from those shown.

Why wouldn't all companies or Business Advisors just use the methods found in the least costly area of the chart? Often times it is not possible. Consider, for example, a new business just starting. Since the business is just starting it has not had a chance to build a reputation. Likewise, it does not have clients yet. So, referrals from business associates or clients may not be a possibility.

New businesses will often be forced to use more costly, less effective ways of obtaining prospects until their business grows and develops.

The essential point is that you know the prospecting opportunities that exist for your business and the cost involved versus the potential of making the sale.

Initial Contact

Success in selling centers on understanding the needs of the customer. The Initial Contact that is made with the prospect provides the opportunity to learn more about the client and his business. It is during this stage of the selling process that you have the chance to strive to uncover the real needs of the client and to begin to establish your credibility as someone who can help satisfy those needs.

Prior to the Initial Contact with the prospect, strive to learn as much as possible about the client, their business and the industry in which it operates. The internet, libraries and business associates can be good sources of this information.

During the initial meeting, you should strive to:

- Confirm the information that was gathered prior to the meeting.

- Understand the business structure and organization.
- Define who the key decision makers in the company are.
- Learn the history of the business and the future plans and objectives.
- Uncover the major issues that the client is facing.
- Build empathy and credibility with the client.

Identifying Needs and Solutions

The ability to make the sale often times hinges on the ability to uncover the true needs of the prospect. This is often a challenge even with prospects willing to speak freely and answer your questions. Prospects often do not know or understand their true needs or problems. Apparent problems may be the symptom of greater problems that must be resolved to permanently resolve the issues. To bring value to the client, you need to direct the client's attention to the greater problem and help them to realize the benefit of resolving this problem.

One of the main objectives of this portion of the selling process is to uncover the prospect's or client's main areas of concern. Once these are identified, it provides the opportunity to begin discussing solutions with the client. This, in turn, provides the opportunity to begin developing credibility with the client and to exhibit empathy for the problems being faced. At this point, it is also a good time to provide examples of how other businesses having similar problems have been helped.

Through out this process, you should be looking for areas in which to provide immediate value. One of the fastest ways to begin establishing credibility with a client is to identify additional problems that the business may be facing, and offering effective solutions.

Uncovering the client's main concerns and identifying possible immediate problem areas will highlight obvious areas of concern in the business. This presents a good opportunity to explain the need for a more detailed needs assessment at the appropriate time.

A *Needs Assessment* looks at each area of the client's business and evaluates the systems and procedures currently in place. There are several *Needs Assessment* tools available to assist in completing this process, including the one available from Business Excellence Partners.

Overcoming Objections

One of the common mistakes that sales people and Business Advisors make is assuming that the client understands the suggestions that are being made. This is very often not the case. The objections that a client raises often serve to clarify the misunderstandings or omissions.

The first step in overcoming objections is to LISTEN. Once a client raises an objection; it is not the time to be defensive. It is an opportunity to learn what the client may have misunderstood in your presentation.

The objection should be ACKNOWLEDGED and respected because it represents the client's feelings. A client will only buy when you satisfy their needs. Objections indicate that the client does not fully understand how the suggestion you have made will satisfy their needs.

Objections provide the opportunity to once again show that you can EMPATHIZE with the client and the problem being faced.

When objections arise it is a time for clarification. One approach is to restate the problem being addressed. Then restate the solution being suggested. This will ensure that both you and the client see the problem and solution the same way. You should also use this time to emphasize the danger of taking no action.

The key to effectively handling objections is to LISTEN and LEARN.

Closing

As the selling process progresses it should follow a logical order. First, the client's need is uncovered. Then it is determined how the client intends to handle the issue. Next a solution is presented. Then objections are addressed. And, finally, the client realizes that he needs YOU to effectively solve the problem.

If any of the steps are omitted or not fully addressed, the sale will not be made.

If all are presented properly, the sale will almost close itself. Watch for the buying signals throughout the presentation. Buyers often nod their head in agreement. Or they ask questions like "if we decide to do this, when could you begin?" But the phrase we strive for most is **"Can You Help Me With That?"** This simple phrase demonstrates that you have developed credibility, confidence and empathy with the client.

Sometimes, even if everything is presented properly, the client fails to ask for help. If this happens, remember that it is always okay to Ask For The Order.

Tracking

As the Sales Process chart shows, the sales process does not end with the closing of the sale. Selling needs to be an on going process.

Many businesses only think about sales when sales are down or non existent. Sales needs to be an **everyday activity**!

Many successful businesses and Business Advisors develop a tool for tracking future sales. Think of future sales as a pipeline. Your ability to keep the pipeline full will ensure future success. Most businesses think only about sales that have already been made. The focus needs to be on what is in the pipeline and what is coming.

There are tracking forms available, you can develop your own, or you can use the one from Business Excellence Partners. The essential thing is that you begin immediately to track your future success.

Summary

Understanding the Sales Process is important to you if your practice is going to grow and succeed. Each of us, whether we view ourselves as "salespeople", or not, play a role in the selling process for our companies. Each time we interact with a client or prospect we sell in some way. Understanding the Sales Process helps us to be more effective in this effort.

As the diagram in this chapter reflects, the Sales Process can be thought of as a circle. It is ongoing. When a sale is lost, it is usually because the Sales Process has been stopped before the circle has been completed.

Our goal throughout this book is to provide a model, that when followed, will result in a successful, sustainable Business Advisory practice. This cannot be achieved without an effective Sales Plan. Developing your Sales Plan relies on your understanding of the Sales Process and how each step impacts you and your clients.

Gaining new clients must be a part of each day's activities. Understanding the Sales Process will make that activity easier and will help to ensure that the practice you are building will remain "Fully Booked".

BUSINESSEXCELLENCE

Chapter 6- Keeping The Pipeline Full
By Chuck Thompson

"How's your business? Great, I had sales last month of $50,000." Too often we judge the health or performance of our businesses by what has happened in the past. But often, what has happened in the past is not a sure sign that business will continue at that level in the future. A better indication might be... anticipated orders in the future. Many businesses do not have any idea what the future holds in terms of potential sales. They just "hope" that things will continue as they have in the past.

In this chapter, we will conclude the Sales Plan topic, and the "No Vacancy" level of our model, by discussing the importance of your sales Pipeline and a tool to monitor it.

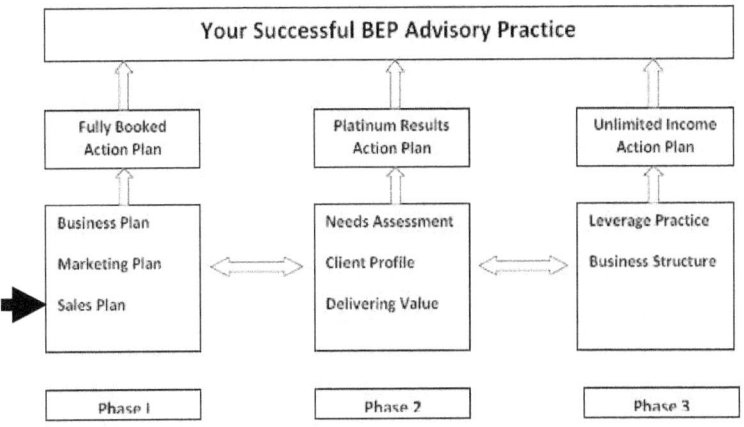

Knowing what will happen in the future is important to every business. If we can accurately predict future sales it allows us to take the necessary steps to profitably run our operations. Important things like ensuring that we have the necessary inventory or raw materials to match sales demand and that we have sufficient cash to finance our growth and manpower to staff the operation. Every area of business relies on accurate sales forecasting to direct future actions. And, it is equally important for the Business Advisor.

The Sales Pipeline

The sales pipeline continually supplies sales to the business advisor. It can be thought of as the major blood vessel that keeps your business alive. If the pipeline is not kept full, eventually your practice will falter. So, the question becomes, how can you ensure that your pipeline is kept full?

Most business advisors monitor sales performance by comparing actual sales (shipments) versus a budget or the previous year. While this is a valid measure, it only tells part of the story. Successful advisors also measure expected future sales. By doing so, they are able to anticipate if they will meet their future plans and projections.

The sales pipeline can be monitored through the use of a tracking tool or tracking program. These are available from many sources depending on the level of complexity needed. A simple and practical tool for business advisors is available from Business Excellence Partners. It is easy to use and provides all the detail that you need to monitor the future activity of your practice. Visit http://businessexcellenceworkshops.blogspot.com/ for more details.

The tracking tool monitors anticipated orders by customer. Once a sales presentation is made or a quote is given, information is entered into the Pipeline monitoring tool for tracking. For each entry, expected sales volume is recorded and a probability of getting the assignment, or landing the client, is assigned along with an anticipated order date. The tracking tool, then, will monitor open activity based on probability and calculate potential future order volume. Remember, your goal is to stay "Fully Booked", so your Pipeline volume needs to at least match your budgeted sales volume for the period.

The following example and the chart below, shows how a Tracking Tool might work for the

Business Advisor. In this example, the Business Advisor is working on developing existing clients, but also trying to add new clients. In January, the Business Advisor contacted two existing clients and two potential clients and gave quotes to each of them. If client #1 decides to work with the Advisor, the order will be for $12,000 and will be placed in May. At this point, the Advisor feels that the he has a probability of 50% of getting the order. Client #2 is much more certain. They have an immediate need. The quote given was for $10,000 and would be placed in March. The probability of getting this order is 80%.

Prospect #3 received a quote of $8,000. If they place the order it will be in April. The probability now is 40%. Prospect #4 received a quote of $25,000. They too will place the order in April if they decide to order. The probability is 30%.

Using the information above, and the Business Excellence Partners Tracking Tool, the Business Advisor's future earning potential might look like this:

PIPELINE FOR:	Joe – Business Advisor					10/30/2009		

	Total value of Pipeline:	$55,000		Expected value of Pipeline:		$24,700		

OPPORTUNITY	STAGE	NAME/CLIENT	$ VALUE	START DT	EXP.CLOSE	% CHANCE	Exp. VALUE
Client #1	Early	Jones	$12,000	5/15/10	8/1/10	50%	$6000
Client #2	Advanced	Wilson	$10,000	3/1/10	6/1/10	80%	$8,000
Prospect #3	Intermediate	O'Reilly	$8,000	4/15/10	5/15/10	40%	$3,200
Prospect #4	Intermediate	Larson	$25,000	4/18/10	10/1/10	30%	$7,500
							$ -
							$ -
							$ -
							$ -

For the tracking tool to be effective it must be continually updated as conditions change. The probability is increased or decreased based on future discussions with the client or prospect. Orders received are removed from tracking. Likewise, orders lost are also removed.

As discussed in the previous chapter, how sales are obtained can differ for a Business Advisor who may be just starting a practice versus an Advisor who has been in business for many years. However, the need to track future potential business does not change. For the new Advisor, future orders will probably be generated by landing new clients. For the established Advisor, the majority of orders will probably come from existing clients. The tracking concept remains the same. The difference could lie in what exactly is tracked.

The new Advisor would track potential business from prospects. Similar to the example above, the established Advisor may track specific jobs or types of orders because an existing client may have several different projects throughout the year.

For sales pipeline tracking to be effective it must be monitored and utilized. The concept of focusing on future orders must become an integral part of the thinking of the successful Business Advisor.

How much potential sales volume should be in the pipeline at any given time? The answer will differ for every Business Advisor depending on the desired income from their practice. It will also be dependent on the average number of quotes you successfully close. If historically you close 50% of the quotations submitted you will need to maintain a sales pipeline equivalent to twice the sales you are trying to achieve. Over time, as you begin working with a Tracking Tool, patterns will develop and you will be able to estimate your sales closing ratio.

Selling is a business. It does not just happen by luck. If you utilize the many tools available your probability of success will greatly increase. Tools like the Tracking Tool just discussed will help to make sales more predictable. Tools like a Needs Assessment will help to uncover additional opportunities for sales within existing clients.

Selling is a business. Like any business it needs constant attention every day. Too many companies and Business Advisors think about sales only when sales are down or non existent. The selling process must become part of the daily routine of the business. A Tracking Tool, focusing on future business, will help to make that happen.

BUSINESSEXCELLENCE

Chapter 7 – Client and Segment Profiles
By Mary Trost

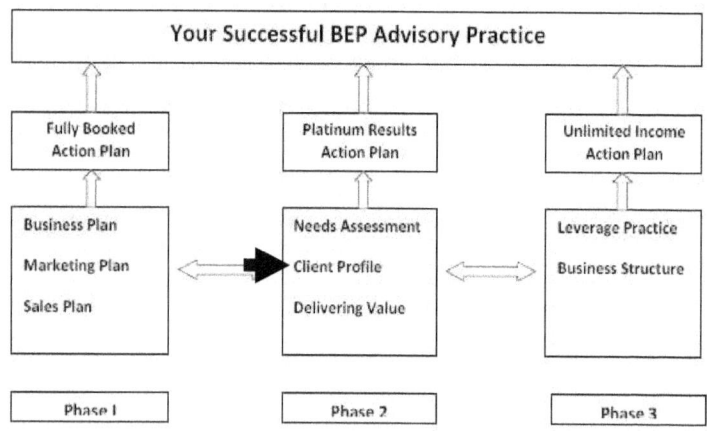

Make Sure the You They Ask is <u>YOU!</u>
Building Trust is the Key to being a Successful Advisor

The key to your success as an advisor is the ability to earn the trust and confidence of your clients. Trust is the foundation of client satisfaction and loyalty. Technical mastery of your discipline is not enough for a client to hire you or to refer you to someone else. In fact the relationship with a small business owner is less about how well you did your last job and more about what you can do for them. Your job is to convince them that your experience and skills can help them build and maintain a successful business based on their strengths, desires and abilities.

So how do you build trust with your clients? Well, it's not something that usually happens in an instant. Unfortunately, a potential client needs to believe that they can trust you when they interact with you for the first time. So here's a list of some of the characteristics of trust:

Must be earned and deserved – Tell the truth and follow through with anything you say

Grows, rather than just appears – Every time you do what you say you will, trust grows
Presumes a two-way relationship – Realize there are 2 business experts in the relationship
Is intrinsically about perceived risk – Will hiring you be money well spent?
Is different for the client than for the advisor – For you it's a job for them it's their life
Is personal – Business owners need to feel that you are a friend and an advisor

That's a pretty tall order to accomplish in a meeting or two, but there are skills that can demonstrate your trustworthiness to a potential client:

Active Listening - A structured way of listening and responding to others. It focuses attention on the speaker. Suspending one's own frame of reference and suspending judgment are important in order to fully attend to the speaker. The benefits of active listening include getting people to open up, avoiding misunderstandings, resolving conflict and building trust.

Self Confidence - The concept of self-confidence relates to self-assuredness in one's personal judgment, ability, power, etc. When one doesn't possess a belief in their own abilities, it sometimes manifests as over confidence in a business advisor.

Ego Strength - A term used in psychology to reflect a person's overall evaluation or appraisal of his or her own worth. True ego strength allows the business advisor to be able to offer the best solutions to the client.

Curiosity - An emotion related to natural inquisitive behavior such as exploration, investigation, and learning. Authentic curiosity allows the business advisor to see each client as an individual with unique challenges and not prejudge them.

Inclusive professionalism – Acknowledges the skills, abilities and determination of your client as a partner in making the business successful.

Client satisfaction and loyalty depend on your ability to build trust. Once you have established your trustworthiness you can be assured of more business from your clients and their referrals will help you grow and maintain your advisory practice.

Trust should be a cornerstone of your Business Advisory Brand.

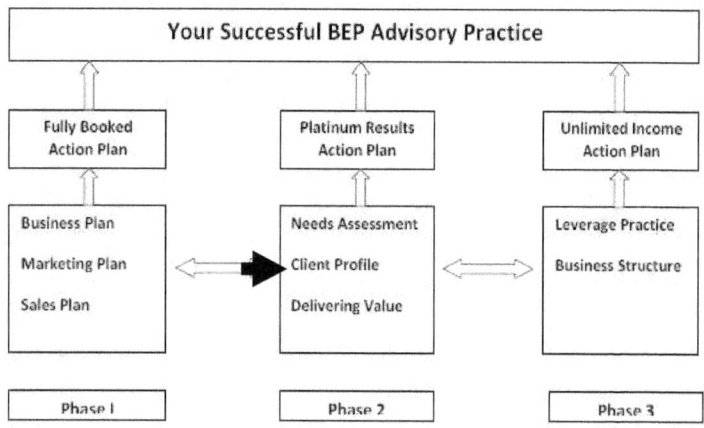

Getting to Know You. . . getting to know all about . . .Yourself

In the first section of this Chapter we talked about the importance of Trust in building your practice.   We   outlined   some   of   the

Characteristics of Trust and listed some of the skills you need to demonstrate your Trustworthiness. In this section we will talk about the need for you to know your inherent strengths and weaknesses and your dominant communication style.

If you are moving from a top management position where people do what you say because you are the boss to work as a business advisor where you are NOT the boss, a personality assessment may be in order. You will learn your dominant communication style and how it affects attracting clients who are like you and those that have different dominant communication styles. This might be quite difficult, because the skills you use as a successful supervisor aren't the same skills you will need as a successful Business Advisor. However, once you are aware of your strengths and weaknesses, you can work to develop or minimize them in order to develop good working relationships with clients or potential clients.

A personality assessment will help you identify your own biases and minimize them so that you can express appreciation for the diversity of lifestyle and needs of your clients, invite diverse perspective, personalize your style and respect differences. By studying the different characteristics of the different communication styles you can learn to quickly determine the probable dominant communication style of a potential client and you can quickly adjust your style to build rapport. An assessment tool that we use and recommend is The InnerView© by The Carefree Institute. In our experience this instrument offers you much more valuable information for you than others we have tried. Go to our website: http://bepinnerview.blogspot.com/ for information on how to purchase this tool.

For purposes of this example we will use the personality descriptors of the InnerView Assessment Tool©. There are four main communication styles:
- Dominance

- Interactive

- Steadiness

- Compliance

Here is a brief description of each of the styles:

Dominance: People who score high in the intensity of the "D" styles factor are very active in dealing with problems and challenges, while low "D" scores are people who want to do more research before committing to a decision. High "D" people are described as demanding, forceful, egocentric, strong willed, driving, determined, ambitious, aggressive, and pioneering. Low D scores describe those who are conservative, low keyed, cooperative, calculating, undemanding, cautious, mild, agreeable, modest and peaceful.

Interactive: People with high "I" scores influence others through talking and activity and tend to be emotional. They are described as convincing, magnetic, political, enthusiastic, persuasive, warm, demonstrative, trusting, and optimistic. Those with low "I" scores influence more by data and facts, and not with feelings. They are described as reflective, factual, calculating, skeptical, logical, suspicious, matter of fact, pessimistic, and critical.

Steadiness: People with high "S" scores want a steady pace, security, and do not like sudden change. High "S" individuals are calm, relaxed, patient, possessive, predictable, deliberate, stable, consistent, and tend to be unemotional and poker faced. Low "S" intensity scores are those who like change and variety. People with low "S" scores are described as restless, demonstrative, impatient, eager, or even impulsive.

Compliance: People with high "C" styles adhere to rules, regulations, and structure. They like to do quality work and do it right the first time. High "C" people are careful, cautious, exacting, neat, systematic, diplomatic, accurate, and tactful. Those with low "C" scores challenge the rules and want independence and are described as self-willed, stubborn, opinionated, unsystematic, arbitrary, and careless with details.

You can see that once you familiarize yourself with the characteristics of each of the types, you will have a good idea how to determine which style a potential client may be in the first or second communication.

Once you know your style and have a good idea of your Client's style you will need:
- A Model for "adapting" your style to more closely mirror/support your Client's Style

- Plan future meetings with your strategy in place
- Evaluate the success of the Interaction
- Make adjustments if necessary

The following chart is an example strategy of how an Advisor with a high dominant style could adjust their style to better work with other styles.

Your Dominant Style	How To Work With Different Styles
High Dominance	**If they are a High Interactive:** Focus more on feelings, Don't overdo facts and logic, make personal contact, don't box them in, need freedom.
	If they are a High Steadiness: Slow your pace, don't rush decisions or force deadlines, don't come on too strong, provide detail, be accurate, listen carefully.
	If they are a High Compliance: Slow your pace, provide structure, focus on feelings, listen, be supportive.
	If they are another High Dominance: Avoid power struggles, negotiate, listen, be less assertive

In addition to understanding different communication styles, you need to know about the diversity in the different generations of business owners. Currently there are four generations of business owners with very different ideas and work ethics in the workplace. In order for you to be successful as a Business Advisor, you must be aware of the generations and their preferred way of doing business. The generations currently in the workplace are:

Traditionals born before 1946
Baby Boomers born between 1947 and 1964
Generation X born between 1965 and 1977
Generation Y, born between 1978 and 1990

Each generation has very different lifestyle and workstyle characteristics as a group and individually. To give you an idea of the differences, here are few examples of the how the different generations approach work in general.

	Traditionals	Baby Boomers	Gen X	Gen Y
Work Ethic	Dedicated	Driven	Balanced	Determined
View of Authority	Respectful	Love/Hate	Unimpressed	Polite
Attitude About Change	Distrust	Believe the World Can Change	Bring It!	Accepting
Preferred Leadership Style	Hierarchy	Consensus	Competence	Together

To help explain the differences in a simple manner, let's use this scenario:

A big project has come to your department, but there needs to be a lot of extra time spent on it to get it done well and on time. You decide to offer overtime for those who work extra time on the project. The response from staff from the different generations may look like this based on "Work Ethic" traits:

Traditionals: *Will put aside other work and focus on the project, will usually work overtime if it is necessary.*

Boomers: *Will put their other work and their personal life aside to complete the project. Will expect the overtime pay in the next paycheck and recognition for their work.*

Gen Xers: *Will work hard during work hours and turn down working overtime.*

Gen Yers: *Will work with dedication and determination and may work overtime.*

You may meet business owners in all of the generations in your practice. By understanding these different work traits you can tailor your communication, presentations, data and your expectations to each specific client in a way that is most acceptable to them.

Business Advisors wishing to remain successful in the future must not only create a work and communication style that supports and includes the diverse styles that reflect business owners, but understand the differences between the generations of business owners.

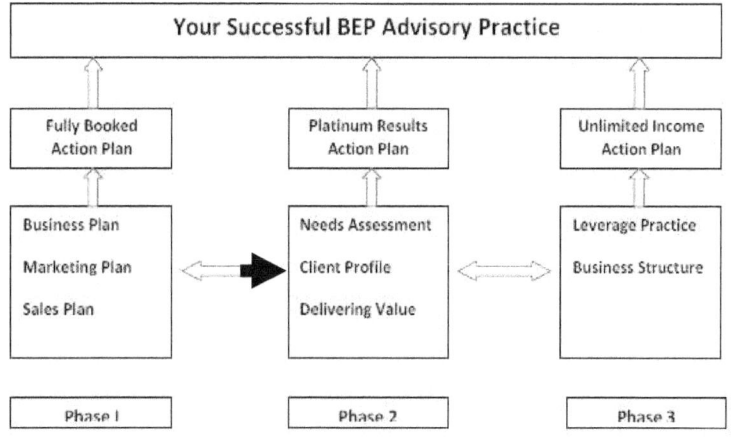

Your Successful BEP Advisory Practice		
Fully Booked Action Plan	Platinum Results Action Plan	Unlimited Income Action Plan
Business Plan Marketing Plan Sales Plan	Needs Assessment Client Profile Delivering Value	Leverage Practice Business Structure
Phase I	Phase 2	Phase 3

Getting to Know You . . . . getting to know all about Small/Medium Businesses

Small/Medium businesses are very different from large corporations in almost every way you can imagine. They are similar in that they both want to be successful and profitable. In the previous section of this chapter we talked about the need for a Business Advisor to be able to recognize their own dominant communication style and that of their client or potential client and have a strategy for working together that builds a successful relationship. Further, we learned that each generation of business owners could have different attitudes and preferred ways to work than ours. If that isn't enough, we now have to be aware of how different all aspects of a small/medium business can be from those of a large corporation.

The following chart describes some important ways that corporate and entrepreneurial management differ:

	Corporate	Entrepreneurial
Profit	Profit is pre-planned with definite dollar targets determined:	Profit seen as directly related to sales only. Residual profit.
Planning	Precisely defined, systematic forecasting and planning • Strategic planning • Operational planning • Contingency Planning	Planning informal, erratic and sporadic. • Problem solving • Crisis Management
Organization (Structure)	Clearly defined with job descriptions and detailed organizational form.	Structure informal with overlapping and undefined responsibilities
Control (Management)	System of organized control, based on precise objectives, targets, measures, accountability, evaluation and rewards (punishments). Delegation the rule.	Inconsistent, personalized and seldom objective system of controls. Little or no delegation.
Budgeting (Planning)	Formal criterion set using historical information and forecasted growth	No defined criterion with no follow-up on variances
Leadership	Consultative or Participative in Style	Very personalized. From totalitarian to laissez faire
Culture	Well defined and focused	Loosely defined, extended family
Hiring	Structured formal process, legal issues addressed. Background checks.	No formal process. Hire family members/friends. No planning
Physical Environment	Structured office setting. Newer office equipment, computers and furniture	Random arrangement, older equipment, computers and furniture.

This chart does not hold true for every entrepreneurial business you will work with, but in our experience, most or all of the differences are accurate.

As an Advisor who wants to use their expertise to help a small/medium business improve their efficiency, you may want to jump in enthusiastically with the solution to the operating problems of the business. Many times, however, you can't give a business owner what they need until you give them what they want. What they want is to know that you have listened to them and understand their concerns, that you recognize their achievements, that you see their business as a unique entity and that you have the knowledge and expertise to help them.

Showing respect for the business owner's skills, talents, experience and accomplishments are vital to building a lasting relationship. Until they know you and trust you, you won't be able to convince them to make changes that they don't understand or can't see as beneficial to their business, even if the changes will save their business.

Recognize that most small/medium businesses will never run the way large corporations do, and that's the way most entrepreneurs like it.

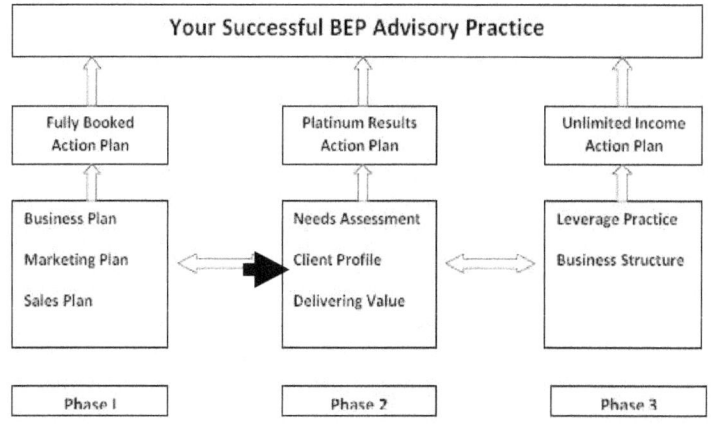

Your Successful BEP Advisory Practice

| Fully Booked Action Plan | Platinum Results Action Plan | Unlimited Income Action Plan |

| Business Plan
Marketing Plan
Sales Plan | Needs Assessment
Client Profile
Delivering Value | Leverage Practice
Business Structure |

| Phase 1 | Phase 2 | Phase 3 |

Getting to Like You . . . . and Hoping You Like Me

The levels of trust over time should increase, and your relationship with a business owner will take on many new facets. The chart below demonstrates how a business relationship moves from Service Based in the beginning to Trust Based after a period of time. Indicators of success move from Deliverables to Personal Trust.

Characteristics of Relationship Levels
From a 2007 Presentation from The
Leeman Group (see page 55)

Characteristics of Different Client Relationships

	Focus Is On	Energy Spent On	Client Receives	Indicators of Success
Service Based	Answers, Expertise, Input	Explaining	Information	Timely, High Quality Deliverables
Needs Based	Business Problem	Problem Solving	Solutions	Problems Resolved
Relationship Based	Client Organization	Providing Insights	Ideas	Repeat Business
Trust Based	Client As Individual	Understanding The Client	Safe Haven For Hard Issues	Personal Trust

Some Business Advisors never reach the Personal Trust level with most of their clients, but at the level of a Relationship Based advisory, the repeat business and referral opportunities sustain the Advisor's practice.

Learning Objectives for this Chapter
An understanding of:
The Key to Successful Client Relationships

The Importance of Knowing Your Personal Strengths and Weaknesses as an advisor - and how to use them to your advantage

Implications of Multigenerational Business Owners for Advisors
A realistic understanding of how most Small/Medium sized businesses operate compared to corporate businesses

Soon your Calendar will say

because

BUSINESSEXCELLENCE

Chapter 8 – The Needs Assessment
An Effective Tool to Deliver Platinum Results
By: Kjell Andreassen, AInstIB, CExP

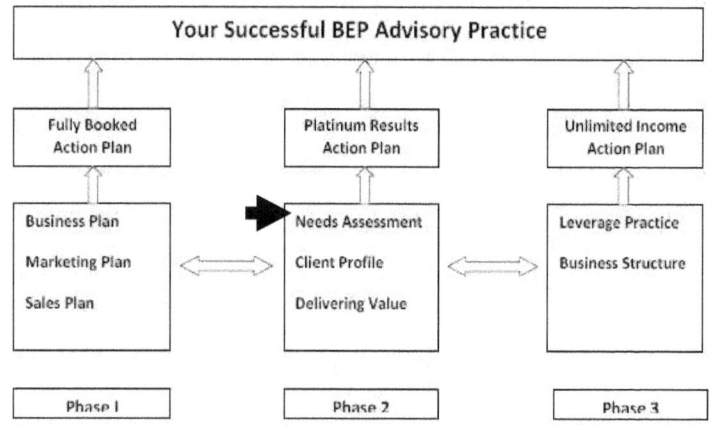

What is a Business Needs Assessment and why do you need one?

As an advisor you are a service provider. The ongoing challenge is to help the business owner client identify the needs and for you as the advisor to show continued results. This will impact the generation of new engagements and prolong existing engagements. A Needs Assessment is a systematic exploration of the way things are and the way they should be. We must determine the current state of affairs, examine the needs relative to the goals of the organization and identify what are the desired or necessary conditions for success. The difference (the "gap") between the current and the necessary will define the needs, purpose and objectives.

By conducting a Needs Assessment we are able to identify causes of performance problems and/or opportunities as well as identify possible solutions and opportunities. The Needs Assessment becomes a valuable tool in the sales process (see chapter 5).

Can You Help Me With That?
A well conducted Needs Assessment with a prospect will help identify areas where you can be of assistance and help you get the engagement.

Ongoing measurements of progress help identify the results that you have achieved (the value that you bring), thus solidifying the engagement and setting the stage for referrals. Ongoing measurement and updates to the Needs Assessment also help identify further needs, areas where you can be of further assistance, thus prolonging the engagement

Techniques for Needs Assessments
There are a number of models and tools available to assist you in performing the Needs Assessment. Some are basic questionnaires in interview format that you can go through with the client. Other models have more advanced support with graphics and financial modeling capability. You can also develop your own, based on your area of expertise, specialty or experience. The objective remains the same; develop a process for identifying gaps and arranging these gaps in priority for resolution. You will demonstrate the needs in a consultative and independent way and have the opportunity to provide solutions and valuable advice – leading to: "Can You Help Me With That!"

Business Excellence Partners has developed a comprehensive tool for a Needs Assessment that is available on its website (http://businessexcellenceworkshops.blogspot.

com/). By going through a series of questions and an assessment of the current state of affairs and the relative importance of a number of areas in the business, this model will produce a graphical representation of the areas you recommend that the business owner address – which gives you an excellent opportunity to provide advice and value.

Assessment Rating
When analyzing the strengths, weakness, and potential of any business there are literally hundreds of functional and operational areas / issues to be considered. There are though, a number of key items that give an indication of the areas that may be draining cash, profits, and potential. These items are listed below to form an analysis of key business points. In performing the analysis, the main ingredient is honesty. Pick the rating category that accurately fits where the item is today.
Here are some basic guidelines for rating

N/A	An area in which there is never a problem or this does not apply to the business.	Perfect or not applicable
1	Is an area that performs well.	Does not cause dissatisfaction at all.
2	Is an area that is occasionally a problem area.	On occasion dissatisfied with.
3	Is a problem area.	Somewhat dissatisfied with.
4	Is a major problem area.	Completely dissatisfied with.
5	Does not exist - major deficiency in the business.	Is never considered. Does not exist in writing.

Any area rated above a two (2) is an area that is operationally deficient and in need of attention/improvement.

Importance Rating
Rate how important each of these areas are to your <u>overall business outlook</u>
N/A   N/A
1   Not Important
2   Somewhat Important
3   Important
4   Very Important
5   Crucial

Assessment Index Score
0.0

Cash Flow and Financial Management

	Strength/weakness	Importance	Overall score
Working Capital	5.0	0.0	0.0
Inventory Turnover	N/A	N/A	
Inventory Management	N/A	N/A	
Collection Procedures	N/A	N/A	
Credit Procedures	N/A	N/A	
Credit Line	N/A	N/A	
Capital Budget	N/A	N/A	
Debt Financing	N/A	N/A	

	Strength/weakness	Importance	Overall score
Planning and Budgeting	0.0	0.0	0.0
Budgets	N/A	N/A	
Variance analysis	N/A	N/A	
Monthly Balance Sheet	N/A	N/A	
Monthly Profit and Loss	N/A	N/A	
Break Even Analysis	N/A	N/A	

Advisor: Joe Advisor
Date: Thursday, August 27, 2009

Broken Distribution LLC

Business Needs Assessment

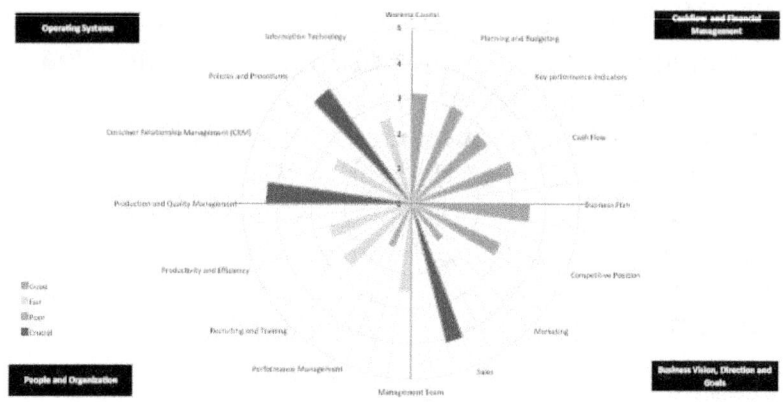

Assessment Index Score

BUSINESSEXCELLENCE

Chapter 9 – Delivering Value
By Mike Tyler

Let's refresh our memory of where we are in relation to our business model; we've completed Phase I and our business plan, our marketing and sales plans and we've been successful in attracting a number of clients. We understand the operating environment and the nature of our client base, and we've seen the value and application of using the tools that have been developed by BEP.

We're at the point in our model where we need to fulfill activities and build a strong reputation for referrals- we need to deliver value to clients!

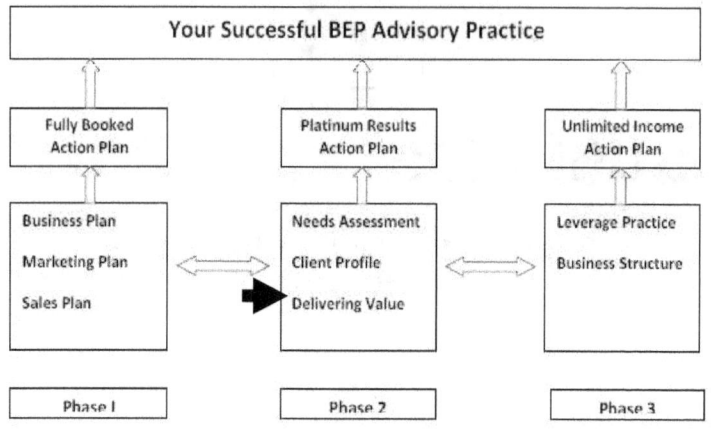

What's Value delivery?

It's amazing how many people do not take the time to ensure that the services they deliver are actually valued by the client. Successfully and consistently delivering value will ensure that you become a trusted advisor, lead to additional referrals and fulfill your particular brand.

Value will have different meaning for different clients, but in the initial client engagement is usually defined by saving the client dollars and/or time or increasing profits. An important issue up front also involves client receptivity, as much as your ability to deliver value.

BEP has developed a value delivery approach that focuses on 4 areas as shown in the diagram below

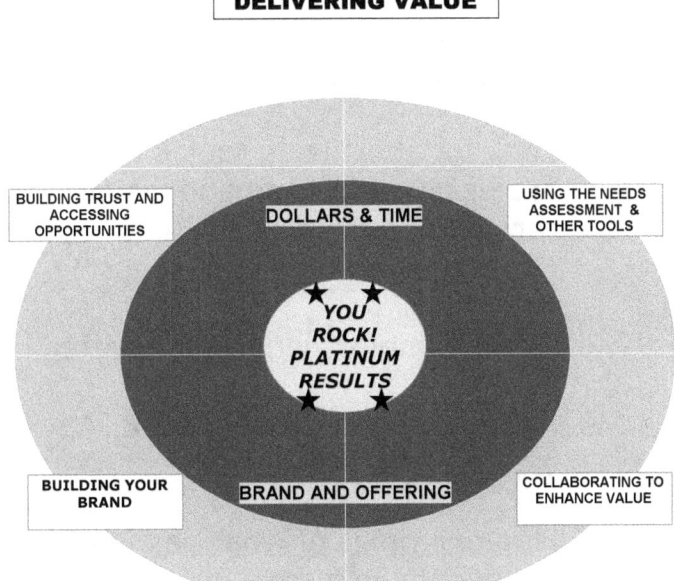

Building Trust and Accessing Opportunities
In the short term the advisor needs to bring practical advice that the client can implement immediately and that will bring short term savings. This in itself will bring credibility with

the owner and their management team, a key
ingredient in gaining access to broader client
opportunities.
Here are a number of guidelines that will help
in this area:

- ▣ Start from the needs assessment with
  something deemed important

- ▣ Look for short term, quick results that
  are easily measured and visible
  throughout the organization
  (Increased sales, reduced cost)

- ▣ Avoid complex, lengthy projects

- ▣ Make sure you deliver; seek "Advisor
  expert" help if necessary

- ▣ Find examples of what has worked within
  the client's industry

The advisor should recognize that they will
need the help of the whole organization in
order to accomplish these short term actions
and actively engage everyone in the process of
developing goals and a plan for
implementation.

Typical areas on which to initially focus include:

(1) Sales
- -Pricing, specific marketing & sales campaigns, unprofitable customers
(2) Direct Costs
- -Purchased material (especially single sourced materials)
- -Overtime labor costs
(3) Expenses
- -Budget controls, telephone costs, insurance costs, leased and rental buildings & equipment,
(4) Cash conservation
- -Working capital reduction, build cash reserves, use supplier financing

These are primary examples but the focus should derive from the output of the needs assessment, as outlined in the previous chapter.

Using the Needs Assessment & other Tools

The results of the needs assessment tool provides a roadmap for how to work with your client and the advisor should work with the client to develop priorities, set goals and assign resources as appropriate. There are other key tools available from BEP that will help with the key areas of business planning, people and organization systems and cash flow projections.

These exceptional and tested tools will bring immediate credibility and allow you to continue to build trust and build your reputation.

Building Your Brand and Collaborating for Success

By defining your own particular brand, as described in Chapter 3 you have created a unique "you"; here's where you get to implement it! This is a danger point and requires focus and discipline not to step outside your brand. There is a tendency for many advisors to try and do everything themselves rather than focus on their "hot spot". They view it as a weakness to bring in another expert advisor, where in reality, it shows strength.

Time and time again clients have been impressed by the depth and breadth of the BEP advisors and it leads to additional business opportunities and referrals.

Bringing in your fellow associates as a virtual Board of Directors is a proven way to enhance your reputation in the eyes of your client, as well as being the most efficient way to implement projects and actions.

Demonstrated Value Delivery
A final word in this area – make sure that what you perceive as value is also value in the clients' minds. It's easy to get wrapped up in focusing on delivering what you believe is value.

BUSINESSEXCELLENCE

Chapter 10- Structuring Your Practice
By Lynn Whitman

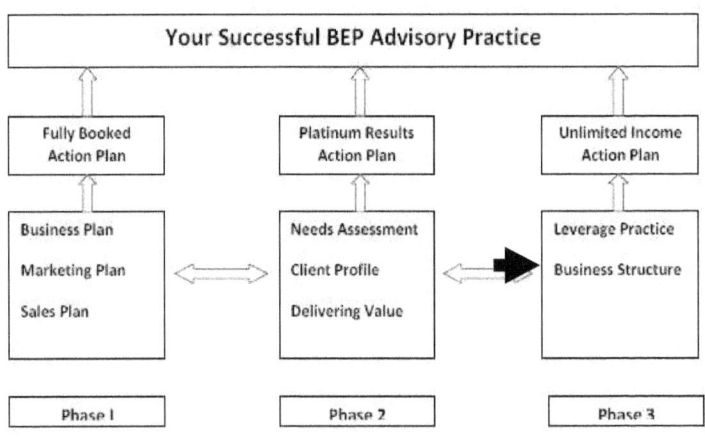

The Nuts and Bolts of Your Business

Business advisors and consultants frequently do not heed their own advice. We tell our clients how important the right structure is for their businesses, yet we give it little thought when it comes to our own business. Many advisory businesses are started with little or no investment. The inner structure (or nuts and bolts) that hold the advisory business together is invisible to the client and for that reason, usually given little thought. However, without the right structure in place, the business will likely fall apart over time. Starting your business with the right structure will help ensure that your business is sustainable and successful. If you are a baseball fan, it's called "loading the bases"!

Legal Structure

Starting with a legal structure, the options for any business are varied. The same holds true for an advisory practice. The practice can be structured as a sole proprietorship, partnership, LLC or a corporation.

Sole Proprietorship and Partnership

There's really nothing *wrong* with operating your business as a sole proprietorship or partnership, but you need to be aware that you will have unlimited liability for business debts. In other words, if your business is sued for any reason, the plaintiff will be able to come after your personal assets, not just business assets.

LLC (Limited Liability Company)

First, there are few tax advantages (or disadvantages) to forming an LLC. In fact, forming an LLC won't change a thing for Federal income tax purposes. Single-owner LLCs are taxed just like sole proprietorships, and multiple-owner LLCs are taxed just like partnerships.

You should, however, be aware that forming an LLC might subject your business to additional state taxes. Certain states (California for instance) subject LLCs to "franchise taxes" in addition to a typical income tax.

The structure of an LLC may provide some liability protection. You should consult your attorney for specific recommendations.

Setting up an LLC is usually fairly simple and can frequently be done without the aid of an attorney. Doing it by yourself is an inexpensive and non-complex option. It is recommended that you seek advice from your accountant (more about this later) prior to setting this up. There are a variety of inexpensive online options that can guide you through this process as well. Legal Zoom (www.legalzoom.com) is a reputable online resource.

S-Corp

S-Corporations have the ability to provide some tax savings as a result of the fact that profits from an S-Corp are not subject to Self-Employment Tax. However, before you're allowed to distribute any profits, you are required to pay any owner-employees a "reasonable salary." This salary will be subject to social security and Medicare taxes (which total the same amount as the Self-Employment Tax). As such, the tax savings only take effect once the business has a pretty sizable income.

Also, you should be aware that S-corporations are significantly more complicated from a tax and legal standpoint than LLCs. So if you form an S-corp, know that you're going to be spending a great many more billable hours with your accountant/attorney.

C-Corp

Unlike most other business structures, C-corporations are taxable entities. This means that the corporation itself is taxed on its income (as opposed to other structures which simply pass the income along to the owner(s), who are then taxed on it).

If you don't plan to distribute all of the profits from your business, you might benefit from forming a C-corp and utilizing a strategy known as "income splitting." The idea is to split the business's income so that part of it is taxable to the corporation and part of it is taxable to the corporation's owner(s), thus putting them each in a lower tax bracket than they'd be in if either one was earning *all* of the income.

The big disadvantage to C-corp taxation is that distributions of profits (known as "dividends") are subject to double taxation. In other words, the corporation is taxed once on its income, and then the shareholders are taxed upon any dividends they receive.

Also, like S-corporations, C-corporations are more complicated from an accounting/tax/legal standpoint than sole proprietorships, partnerships, or LLCs. As such, C-corp owners tend to incur fairly high legal and accounting costs.

Physical Space

Once you have the legal and accounting structure of your business set up, you should consider your physical space. Many advisors choose home offices. Other options are full offices, shared space, executive offices or some combination of these options.

Home Office

For an advisor who is starting his or her practice, a home office may make the most sense. Setting aside a room or work area that is solely dedicated to your business is the optimal situation. In order to be productive in a home office it is important to have everything you need in one place, to minimize distractions and to be focused. Home offices don't work well for people who cannot ignore the distractions that are typically in our homes (barking dogs, piles of laundry, other people in the home etc.) You have to be focused and intent upon the task at hand. It does make a nice commute...and working in your bunny slippers is just fine!

Besides the distraction factor, a big drawback for the home office is the lack of space in which to meet clients, colleagues or others. You can sit down and talk at the dining room table, but your professional image may suffer. Most advisors who have home offices meet clients/colleagues at offsite locations – either the local restaurant/coffee shop or at a facility that has these kinds of spaces available for a fee. The best solution for this issue is to have friends and colleagues who will share their conference room space.

Executive Office

Many business advisors find that they are unable to tune out the day-to-day distractions of working at home and that they prefer the professionalism obtained in an office. Executive suites offer this kind of environment. Most executive suites offer a receptionist, a conference room and possibly office machines, including fax, copier etc. In addition to the physical space and "things", an executive suite situation offers people. Many advisors feel isolated without the interaction with other people. Coming from a corporate environment, many need that human connection to stay creative. This may be especially true if you have recently re-located or have few outside interests.

Executive office spaces abound in larger metropolitan areas. In most cases you can find space that is near your home and competitively priced. Check with colleagues, chambers of commerce, ads and simple drive-bys for something that fits your needs. In comparing prices, be sure to include the extras like office machines, receptionists etc. to be sure you land in a space that meets your needs. Many of these spaces are available without long term leases, allowing you some flexibility.

Outside Office or Shared Office Space

Your own network is the best resource for these kinds of spaces. Make your needs known in the places you network, including clients, friends and colleagues. Sharing space with other business advisors is a great way to collaborate. Sharing space with other kinds of businesses may also enhance your advisory practice. An accountant, insurance agent, lawyer or other service provider may be able to refer their clients easily to you if you are in the same space. (Of course this is true if you are not in the same space as well.)

All office spaces (including a home office) will likely require some small investment, including telephone/fax lines, computer connections or other expenses. Be sure that you keep appropriate records of any expenditure made for office facilities.

Financial and Tax

Many business advisors are guilty of the "Do what I say...not what I do" adage ...usually applied to parenting! Much of what we advise our clients about is financial structure, yet we are lacking a financial structure for our own businesses.

Planning

Start with a plan. Plan the net income you need to make the business viable. Start with a 6 month plan. As your business becomes more viable, build an annual plan, then a 5 year plan. Your business plan will become more important as you develop your revenue streams. (More about this to come). Business plans paralyze many who attempt to write them. There are many business planning software tools out there, including Business Plan Pro. Start simple, use a one page business plan initially and build on it from there.

Below is a quick Business Plan Outline that works for many businesses including a business advisory practice.

1. Consider your company's vision, the big picture. Make it relevant for its purpose, and write "Vision" for the first category with a statement or bullets describing what you envision for the business.

2. Note the mission for the company under "Company Mission." Focus the mission content with the vision and include what the business does, how and whom your company serves.

3. Write "Marketing Strategies" next and describe strategies for growth, service and opportunities involving products and customers. Think of points that reflect the vision and mission as set out.

4. List under "Financial Objectives" a one-year projection of costs and income and write what metrics you'll employ to gauge the success of the objectives with dates.

5. Enter in "Plans" the timetable for development, hiring, fund raising, future location of the business and product rollout.

6. Go over the one page business plan to make it concise with proper grammar and spelling.

7. Keep your business plan fluid by reading it over each quarter. If conditions change, re-consider certain objectives to see if tweaking brings better success.

Budgeting

Put a budget down on paper. I have spoken to many small business owners who tell me that they have a budget. When I ask to see it, they tell me that it is all in their heads. Write your budget down. It needn't be complicated (quick books or other software). It can be as simple as a straightforward excel spreadsheet. Budgets are meant to be changed. It should be changed as often as the situation (both internal and external factors) changes.

In budgeting, include all of your office costs, collateral material costs, communication and equipment. Be sure and include the costs for things that you previously may have used for other purposes (like cell phone costs that you previously considered as personal expenses)

Budgets are best done on an annual basis, but are perfectly useless if you don't review them against actual expenses on a regular (as much as weekly) basis. Frequent review allows you to make the needed adjustments and take the appropriate steps to change the way you are handling your business.

Financial Advice

Unless you have an exceptionally strong background (like as a CPA) an accountant and/or accounting firm makes sense for most business advisors. An accountant can advise you on the tax implications for your "home office", deductible expenses and business structure.

Finding the right accountant/CPA just might enhance your own business. Many advisors have established relationships with CPAs for their personal situations. Certainly it is possible that this individual is the right one for handling your business. It does, however, make sense to review this relationship carefully.

Many advisors have discussions with several CPAs for two reasons: 1. You need financial services from a professional and 2. CPAs/accountants make great referral partners. Frequently a CPA has a client who needs help in their business...and more than the CPA can offer. Their client needs a business advisor. By building a relationship with a financial professional, the business advisor enhances his or her own business.

Banking Relationships

Bankers are another great source of referrals. Making friends with the local business bankers will almost guarantee referrals from their clients who need help with their businesses. Developing these relationships for business referrals, gives you insight into the programs offered at various banks, bankers who are willing to give great service to your clients and banks that make doing business easier. Once you understand these factors for your clients...it makes deciding on a bank to handle your business easy.

Support

<u>Telephones</u>

Options for phone service are myriad, from multiple lines to a single cell phone. Many advisors have an office phone number (separate line, expense). Some advisors have an office line, a fax number and an 800 line installed. Many advisors live with a cell number that can be forwarded, and all other communications being virtual.

You should fight the tendency to make your office a replica of what you might have had in the corporate world. This is a new world and new technology in communications abounds. I would suggest that to start, just use your cell number. If that becomes burdensome, get something else. Unless your business is nation-wide, an 800 number is probably not necessary. If 800 service becomes critical to your business you can set up virtual 800 service quickly with no installation charges and a reasonable monthly cost. You can likely fax from your computer if that becomes necessary. If not, use the local Kinko's or similar store. You'll save the expense of line installation and monthly charges for a few faxes. Most businesses can scan and email documents.

Your cell phone can be your main phone. Make sure that you have the right plan in place to optimize the expenses incurred.

<u>Website</u>

Many advisors just starting out think a website is an absolute necessity...and maybe it is. There are a lot of very successful business advisors out there without a website and many who will tell you that a website is critical. Consider what you want your website to do for you.

Do you want a website to drive traffic to your business?

While this may be a desirable goal, this is a very complex business and requires a well designed plan that includes using the right words in the site, reaching the right audience and some sort of advertising.

Is your website just an image of your business?

There is something to be said for having a website that simply legitimizes your business. In networking and social business situations you may frequently be asked for your website address. Many potential clients will look at your website before calling you. Having a web address on your business is a mark of legitimacy (although this is obviously more perception than reality). This option assumes that YOU direct the traffic to your site.

You can spend anywhere from $200 to $10,000 on a website, plus $100 per hour for changes and upgrades. It can be a very pricey project if not handled appropriately.

As your business matures, it will likely change and your focus or specialty will likely change. In order to make sure that your website changes with your business you need to plan for that eventuality at the inception of your website plan.

One way to ensure that your website is flexible is to use a blog to build your website. The good news on many blogs is that they are free. Blogger.com and wordpress.com both offer very flexible and easy-to-use blogs that can mimic the look of a fully developed website. The best part of using the blog for a website is the flexibility. Blogs can be changed, updated, redesigned...by the user/owner in real time at any time with no associated development fees. If you think blogs are just to share your point of view, consider that you can add videos, pictures, paypal, and many many more options to make your "blog" interesting and pertinent to your business.

Hardware/Software

If you are buying a new computer, a laptop is your best investment. Being able to travel with your computer is critical. Off site presentations are key and wi-fi is all over. With your laptop you can work almost anywhere.

The second outstanding investment is in yourself. Learn how to use your computer and other equipment effectively and efficiently. Take a class, hire an instructor or ask a friend to show you, but take the time to do this.

Don't invest in expensive software up front. Develop your business plan, review your needs, then invest in the kind of software that fits your business. Keep it upgraded and learn to use it well. There is a lot of free, safe software on the web. When you do decide what you need, check out the availability on the web. Ebay also sells some software, and frequently has great pricing.

Make sure you have a decent printer. If you plan to print marketing collateral, consider whether an ink jet or laser best fits your needs. Make sure you have a scanner.

Mail/Ship

If your business includes mailing or shipping packages, most major carriers (including the USPS) offer discounted rates for at-home shipping. By signing up for an internet account (free) you can get discounted rates, print your own labels and just drop packages off at the local office or PO. No more lines at the Post Office!

Free Stuff

There is a wealth of free resources on the web for business advisors. As already mentioned, accounts with mailers/shippers are free (mailing and shipping is not…but they give you a discount). Blogs are free. There are website builders that are free. Some software is free (i.e. Free Open Office- MS compatible software that works like MS Office). There are free .pdf distillers on the web that work great. Great fonts for developing collateral and other uses are available at www.dafont.com.

More…

Survey Monkey – An intro offer is free for small surveys to small groups. You can learn to use the program for free and decide if it is right for your business. It is great for online surveys.

Constant Contact offers a free trial. This is a great resource for client online newsletters. It looks professional and helps you keep in touch with your client base or potential clients. After the trial, you can make a reasonable decision about the value of this for your business.

Skype is free. You can communicate online with other Skype users using voice or voice/video messaging for free. There is some amount of video conferencing that is free within Skype as well.

Conference calling through www.freeconference.com is free. Users pay for any costs associated with dialing in. The basic service is free and provides some amount of reporting for no cost. Upgrades carry a small cost.

VistaPrint offers free printing (you pay only for the shipping) on some products. Business cards are occasionally included in this offering. Check out "free products" on their website at www.vistaprint.com .

The bottom line- lots of resources are available for the "resourceful" business advisor.

BUSINESSEXCELLENCE

Chapter 11-
Leveraging Your Practice
By Lynn Whitman & Mike Tyler

So let's check where we are in the model; we're in Phase 3 and have looked at how to structure and set up our practice. Now we need to understand how to use it to leverage an optimum income.

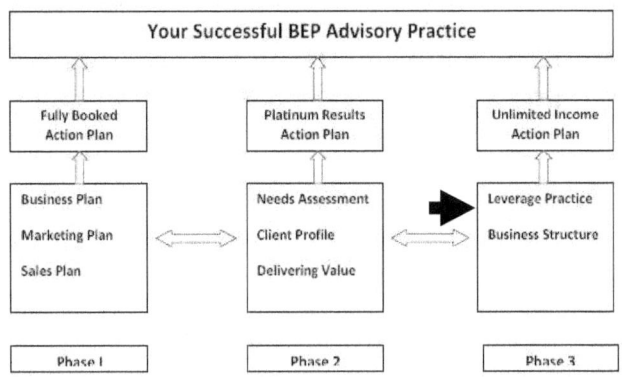

This Chapter deals with two of the key issues that will dictate how well you'll succeed in developing a sustainable, on going practice. The first one deals with developing multiple sources of income which are different in nature and which provide some level of on going income stream. The second issue is one which won't necessarily come easily to the independent minded business advisor- the need to collaborate with other advisors and service providers.

(1)   Developing Multiple Income Sources

Many advisors start this business thinking that they will be able to generate a good living with a handful of clients and a billing rate of $200 per hour.

"Hmmm….that's 30 hours/week (better than the 50 – 60 hours/week I put in at the corporate job) at $200/hour or $6000/week x 46 weeks (I'm taking 6 weeks vacation) = $276,000 per year. Yes, I think I can live on that."

Reality... In order to generate 15 clients to work with you on an hourly basis, you probably need to do 100-150 hours of networking or marketing AND for every hour you spend working directly with a client, you probably need to spend at least an equal amount of time doing prep work or wrap up work. Now you're working more hours per week than the corporate job (lots more!) for less pay....which wasn't exactly the idea when you started out.

So, all things considered, this business model has obvious limitations. The primary limitation is on potential income within available time boundaries. That income ceiling is lower than what most of us imagined was possible. By re-thinking the business model there are many more possibilities. Consider alternatives to the retainer model

You've all heard the caveats about not relying too much on one customer, well the same is also true for market segments, products, investment portfolios etc etc. It's called spreading the risk, and addresses the issue of what happens if you develop too narrow a focus and that particular area develops problems, resulting in reduced opportunities.

What are the other possible income sources?

The business advisor's possible portfolio consists of numerous income generating opportunities such as project work, sub contract work, workshops, seminars and sales of tools and processes to name just a few. Each of these requires a different approach as it relates to planning and implementation, in addition to the resources needed to fulfill them. Also the amount of time and resource needed to generate opportunities will vary greatly depending between the different options. Below is a brief description of the main sources:

Project Work

This is very common where a client is looking for a particular skill or output such as creating a business plan or designing a sales campaign. This type of work may fit in with someone who specializes in a particular area, but also can be useful income for the generalist. Projects can vary in length but typically would last 2- 3 months; referrals are also important here, but this area can require a significant marketing effort.

Sub Contract Work through Collaboration
This generally transpires as a result of collaborating with other advisors and/or providers with whom you have developed a relationship and who perceive you as an "expert" in a particular skill area or discipline. This is an area which is too often ignored by advisors keen to "go it alone" and needs careful attention and management in order to develop key relationships with other advisors and providers, such as lawyers, CPAs and bankers. These relationships will provide referrals and other income opportunities during times when other parts of your business may be in decline and will result in that smoothing effect of your income stream as opposed to the "feast and famine" which is endemic to the industry.

Workshops & Seminars
These are a great way to generate leads as well as provide an on going income stream per se and can be delivered on many subjects. BEP has developed a whole series of 2 hour workshops that can be delivered to groups of up to 40 people and has worked with

Chambers of Commerce and Trade Associations to deliver these to their members. They are an excellent way to build a solid reputation amongst a broad audience and invariably will lead to follow on business with some of the workshop participants. Graduates of BEP's Academy will receive training and materials on how to plan and conduct these workshops.

Books and Webinars

Share your expertise. In today's world, on demand printing makes writing and publishing a book a completely different endeavor than it was only a few years ago. There are many web publishing companies that do not require any up-front investment. Books can be purchased as needed with no prior commitment to quantities. Some marketing and display is offered by the publisher. Under this scenario, a book makes a great statement of expertise and is a usable and effective marketing tool.

Webinars are another great way to use your expertise. Presenting material via webinar offers a revenue generation opportunity as well as a collaboration opportunity. There is a wide variety of software and programs that accommodate webinars. Some are reasonably priced, some are free. A $20 camera and Skype will work in some cases. Webinars are not geographically restricted, so you can use social media efforts to market these opportunities. Webinars, by nature, expend your potential market.

Tools

Many experienced advisors have developed exceptional tools that help them in their client relationships. These tools are as complex as a business needs analysis with a radar graph output (see Needs Analysis) or as simple as the pipeline spreadsheet. All of these tools can be sold to other advisors or clients. In addition there are a number of products in the market place, developed outside the business advisor realm, which can be sold by business advisors. A reliable source of income can be generated by selling a variety of tools to businesses.

This is, by no means, an exclusive list of other opportunities. Advisors have done seminars for chambers and trade associations, developed small business "schools", branched out into more specialized areas and more. The list goes on and on. One thing is true – the effective business advisor utilizes multiple resources and methods to maximize his or her business.

So how do I figure this out?
It would be nice to have a tool that allowed you to play portfolio "what ifs" with the possible different income streams; one that allowed you to see how much effort and number of hours was involved in each activity, versus the reward you would be likely to get. Graduates of the BEP Academy will get such a tool that has been developed based on the actual experiences of the BEP advisors; this proprietary management tool will allow you to develop a realistic view of what it will take to achieve your income goals, as well as make

choices between the various income stream options.

The Table below is an example of an outcome of a series of inputs and choices which will enable a business advisor to map out the varied income sources and the effort required in terms of personal hours required to achieve them. These numbers are purely illustrative and actual achievement will depend on each individual's efforts.

Income Area	# of clients/ projects	Personal Hours per year	Projected Income $000
Monthly retainer	4	1136	96
Consulting Projects	3	276	12
Collaboration	3	444	36
Sales Commission		180	12
Workshops Seminars	2	20	10
TOTAL		2056	166

This matrix represents several means of generating different types of business and an approximation of the hours required to generate clients/projects from each of the different areas. As you can see, the hours in this guide represent almost 40 hours per week for a year (no vacation!!).

Refer back to the "keeping your pipeline full" in Chapter 6 to review the need to keep generating new business all the time.

As you can see, based on these guides, you are unlikely to make a six figure income in the first couple of months of your practice. Over time, your income should increase with fewer hours required to sustain it.

Breaking out the "Monthly Retainer" portion of the income matrix, please review the chart below. This version assumes business is obtained through networking alone. Social networking refers to making the most of the people you already know, as discussed in Chapter 3. 200 hours of calls, meetings, coffee meetings, lunch meetings, discussing you business in a social situation etc. becomes an "all the time" task. This many hours of social networking would likely occur over several months. The same is true for the "join assns" line. As most Chambers, networking groups, etc. meet on a monthly basis, 64 hours of this kind of networking would occur in many groups over 6 or more months. Collaboration through Business Excellence Advisors can occur through face-to-face meetings, telephone/conference call and other kinds of communications, but is still likely to take months to accomplish.

Fee Type: Monthly retainer
Goal: Multiple months of business

		No. Annual Sales	Est. Hours for 1 Sale	Est. Direct Expense	Est. Income
Income					
	Monthly Retainer	4			$ 96,000
Contacts					
	Cold Calls Yourself	0	0		
	Cold Calls outsourced	0	0		
	Direct Mail	0	0		
	Online Mail	0	0		
	Networking				
	>Social Networking	1	200		
	>Join Assns.	1	64		
	>Clients/CBeA	2	104		
	>Personal List	0	0		
Costs					
	Buy a List	0		$ -	
	Hire a Lead Service	0		$ -	
	Direct Mail	0		$ -	
	Online Mail	0		$ -	
	Networking				
	>Social Networking	1		$ -	
	>Join Assns.	1		$ 300	
	>Client/CBeA	2		$ -	
	>Personal List	0		$ -	
Client Time			768	$ -	
Total			1136	$ 300	$ 96,000

(2) Collaborating in order to grow your practice

This area can be counter intuitive for many advisors especially those who have a broad business background and functional experience. In addition, many advisors are concerned about how they will be viewed by their clients if they bring someone else in to handle a specific issue; this is particularly prevalent in the early stages of developing a practice and can result in it taking much longer to establish a sound practice.

Advisors should establish a network of confederates with whom they are comfortable and happy to work; this may only come about as a result of getting to know, and working with, certain individuals.

Graduates from the BEP Academy will have such a network already established and can benefit immediately from the embedded knowledge and experience of existing BEP Advisors. A good way of getting to know other advisors is to set up collaborative projects or ventures in specific areas, such as jointly implementing a series of workshops or developing new offerings. There's no better way of making sure you have the right collaborations than actually working with someone on a real project or activity.

BUSINESS EXCELLENCE

Chapter 12 –
Action Plans and Conclusion
By Mike Tyler

Context of this book
This book will stand on its own, in terms of detailing the actions necessary to build and sustain a successful practice, and is based on the actual experiences of a number of successful business advisors.

The Business Excellence Partners proprietary business model can be followed from the information provided here. However its application is enhanced by obtaining certification from the Business Excellence Workshops. This provides hands on experience in developing and implementing the three phases of the business model. In addition, BEP provides on going support and collaboration for attendees. Interested parties should contact us at info@businessexcellencepartners.com

Developing Action Plans

At this point you have reached the last stage in our model and are ready to develop action plans to implement what you have planned so far.

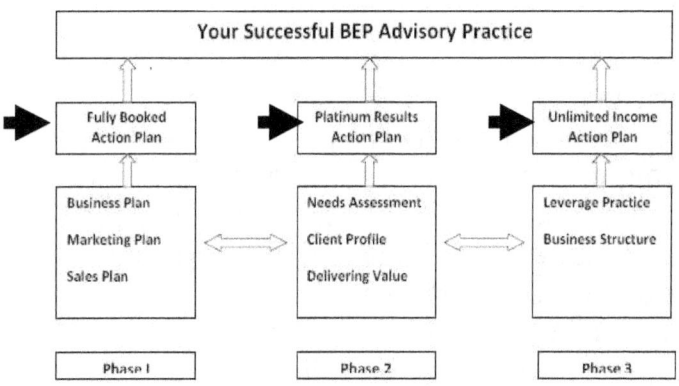

BEP has a tool that brings together all of the required action areas in one document which

makes for easy tracking and measurement. In the last session of the Business Excellence Academy our Advisors work together with Academy attendees to actually generate all the plans they'll need for the next 6 months, so that they walk away with plans they can begin to implement once they leave the Academy. Actual action plans are customized for each individual, and are very detailed, too detailed to outline here, but would include the main areas shown below:

> *Business Plan* – Identify the key areas where there are resource or skill gaps needed to implement your plan and identify what needs to be done to fill them.

> *Marketing Plan-* Start by defining your brand and your hot spot. Develop actions that access your chosen market segment through both direct and indirect marketing; establish actions for building marketing collateral including a web site and a social media strategy.
> Identify and put actions in place for referral networks, other service provider partners and other advisors with whom you can collaborate.

Sales Plan-Define the type of relationship you want to have with your clients.
List the actions you will take daily to identify and get prospects.
Make sure you have your process for identifying problems and suggesting solutions in place.
Prepare a standard sales contract.
Set up your pipeline measurement system.
Set sales goals.

Understanding your clients-Update/develop your personality profile and be prepared to understand your clients' profiles.
Develop different approaches for different profiles.

Legal & Structure-Decide on and set up the appropriate legal structure for your business.
Identify office and equipment needs.
Set up hardware, software and communication systems.
Develop a financial plan.

Conclusion

If this book has given you some insight into the complexities of developing a successful business advisor practice, then it will have achieved its purpose. This is a very rewarding profession, but, as with most things, does not come without experience, knowledge, hard work and perhaps a little help from someone who has done it before.

The principles and ideas presented here are based on the actual experience of successful business advisors, who have operated for many years and the same approach will work for you if you follow the business model. Ultimately you are the architect for your own practice and it will be what you design and build, hopefully this book has provided you with the framework to begin or refine the endeavor.

The tools mentioned in this book are available for purchase at
www.businessexcellenceworkshops.blogspot.com

NOTES

NOTES